THIS BOOK BELONGS TO:

_____

MMG PUBLISHING

Thank you for purchasing this book! If you enjoyed this title any feedback on Amazon would be greatly appreciated. Alternatively if you had any issues, please contact us by email at clunkable@gmail.com

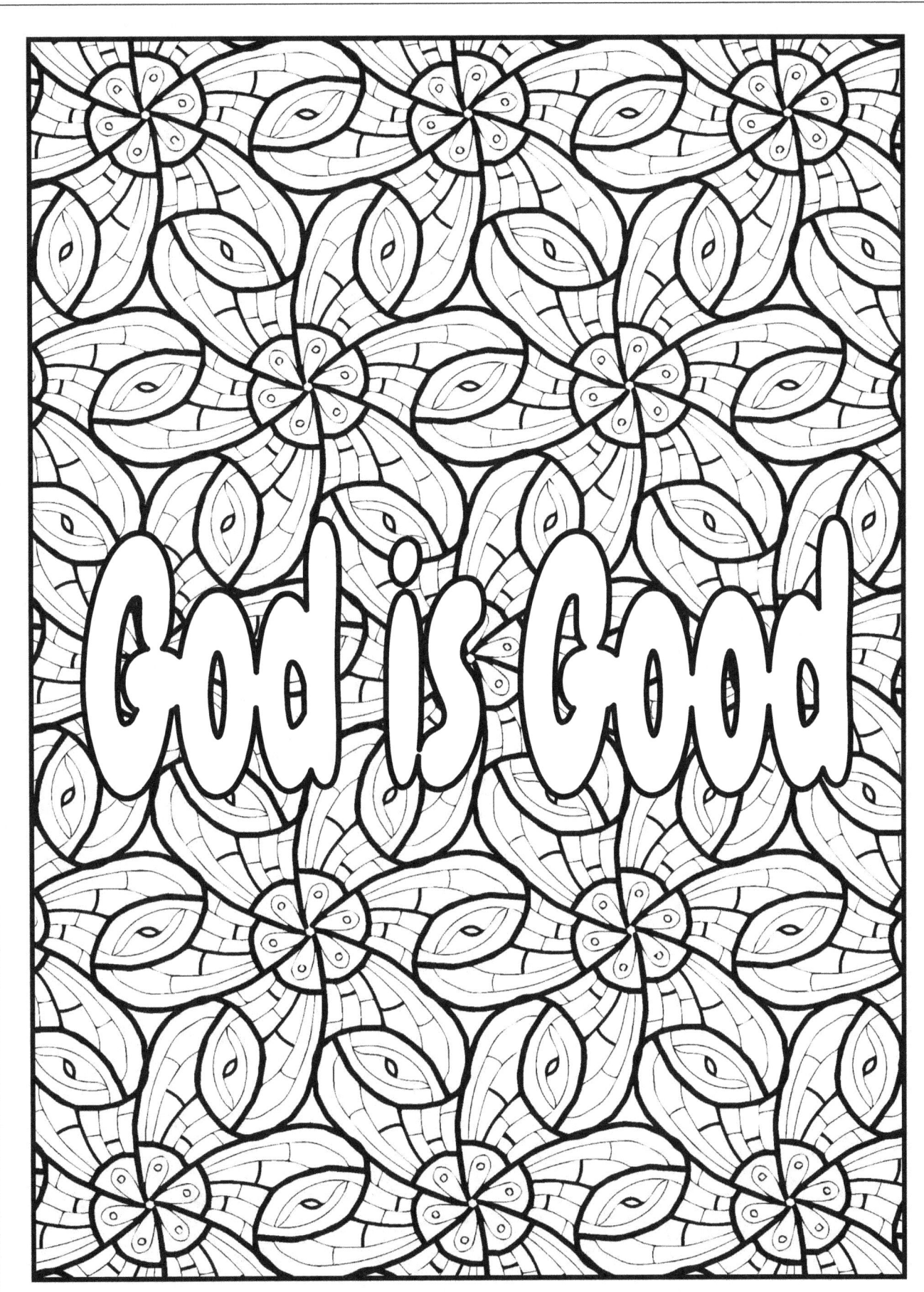

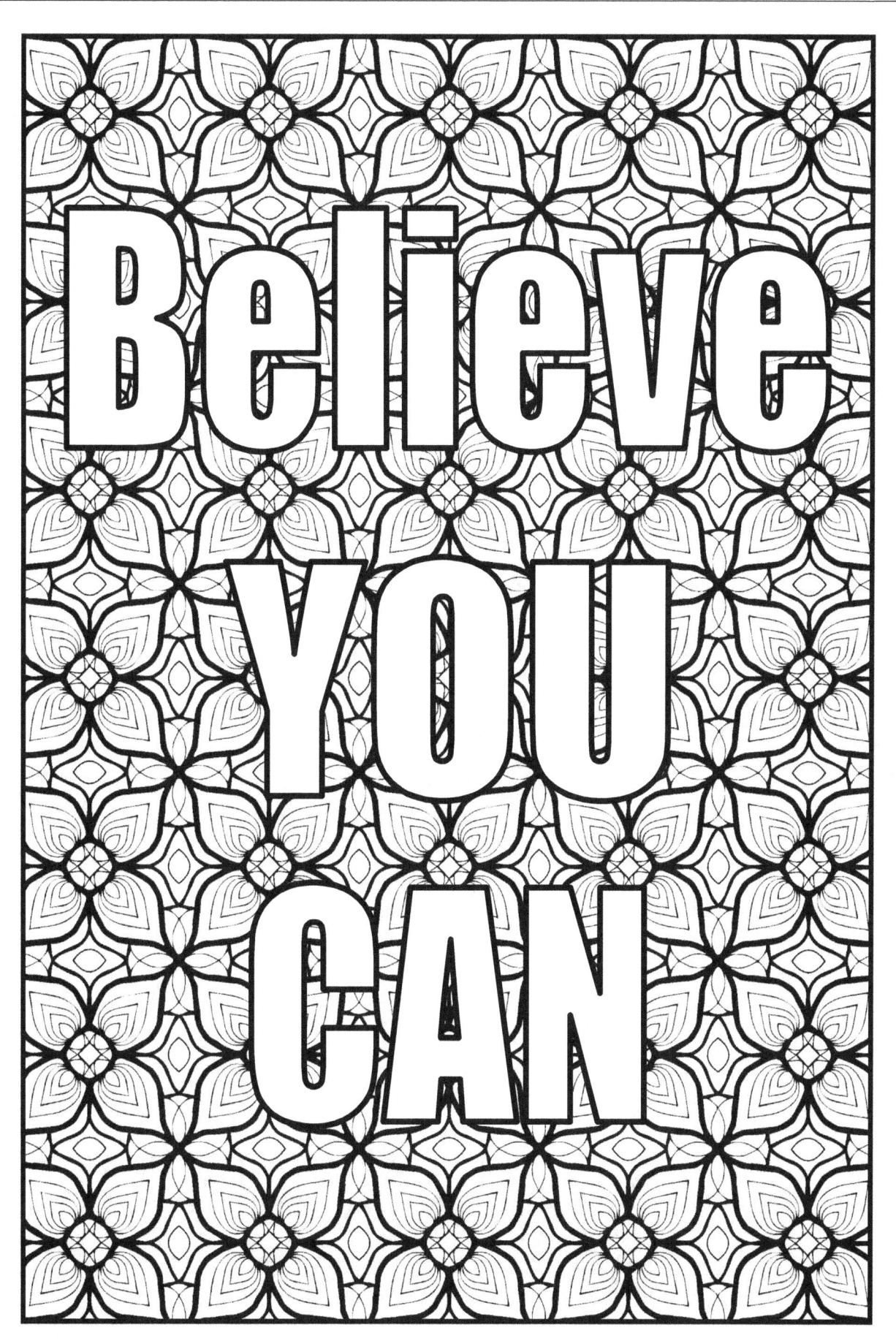

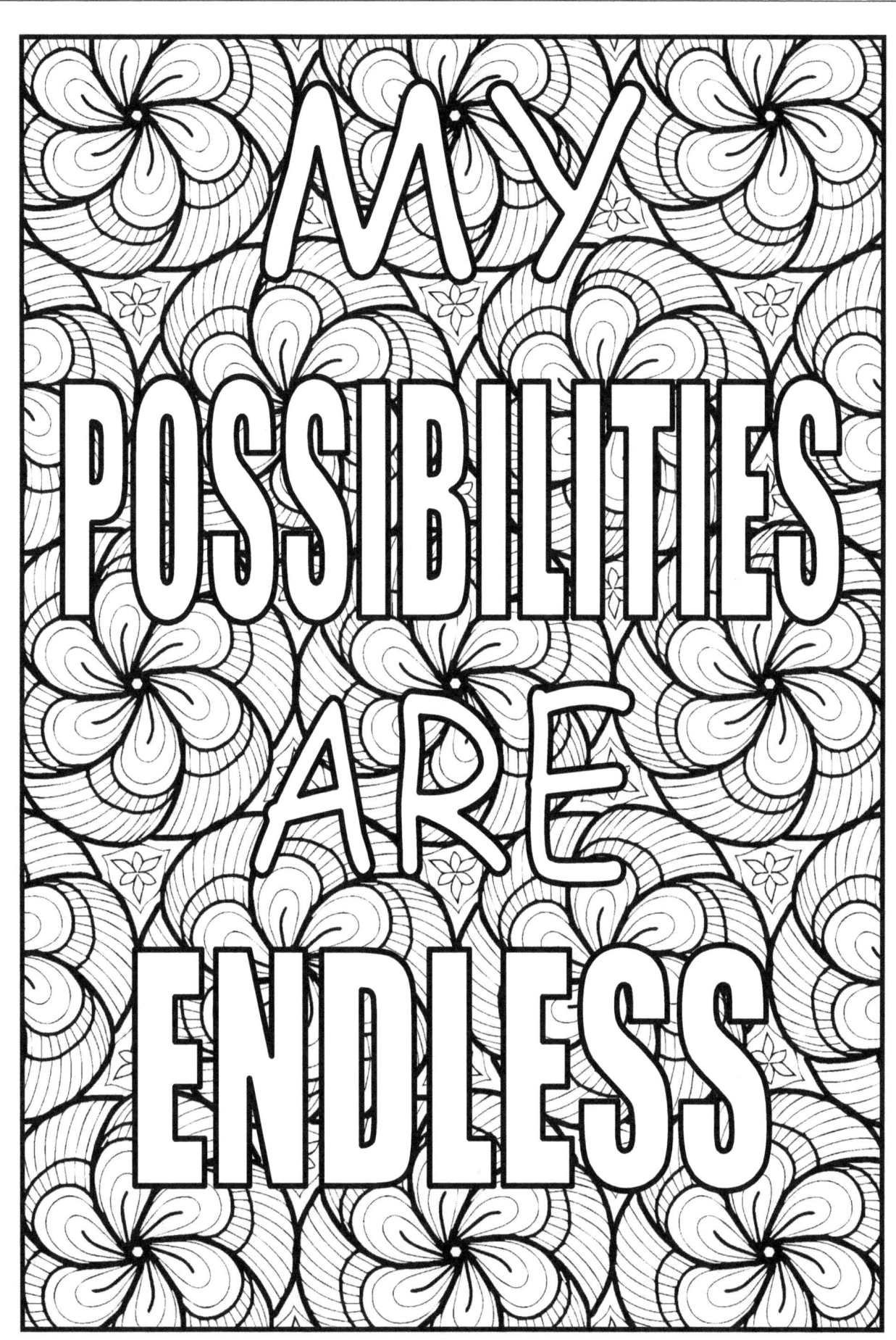

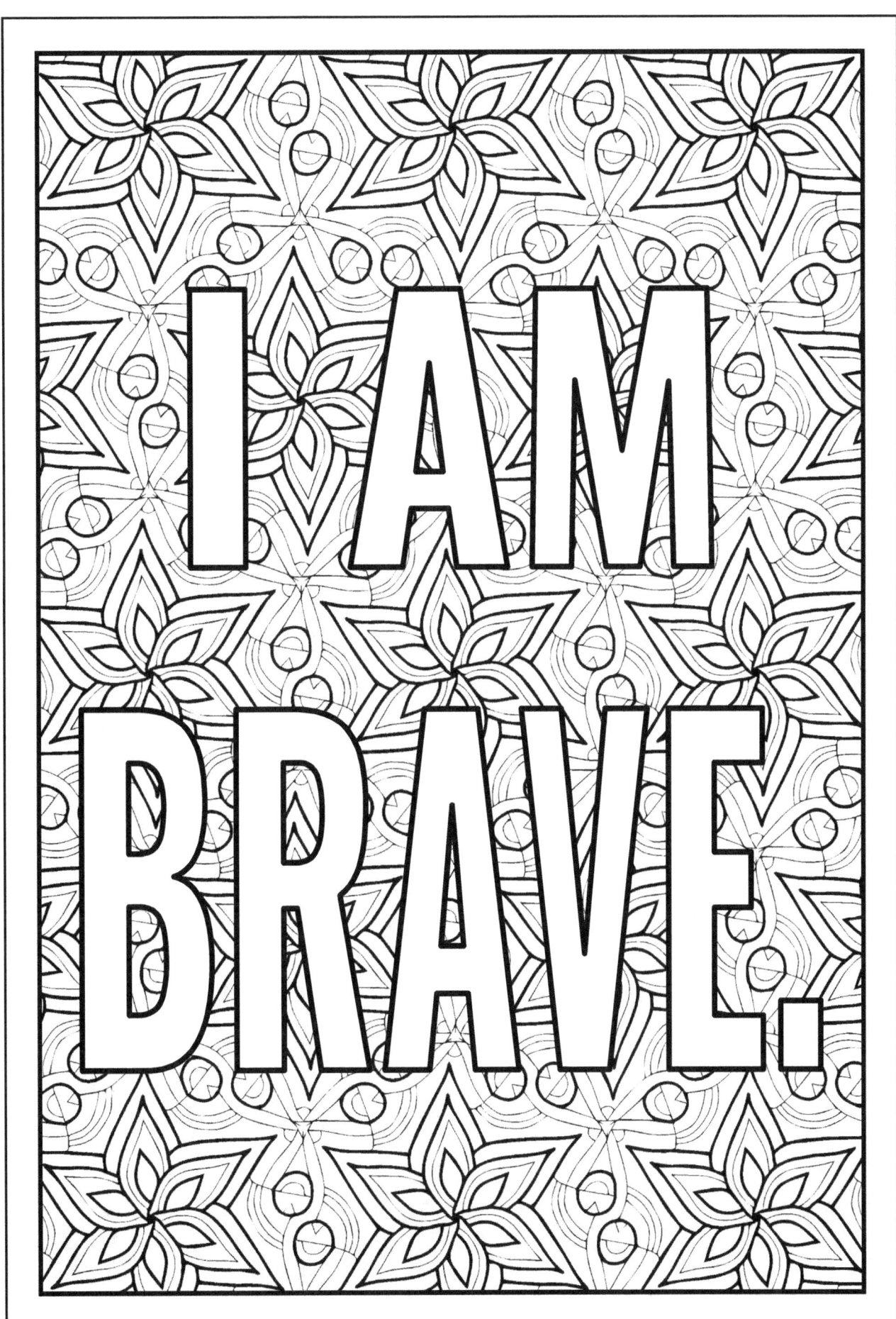

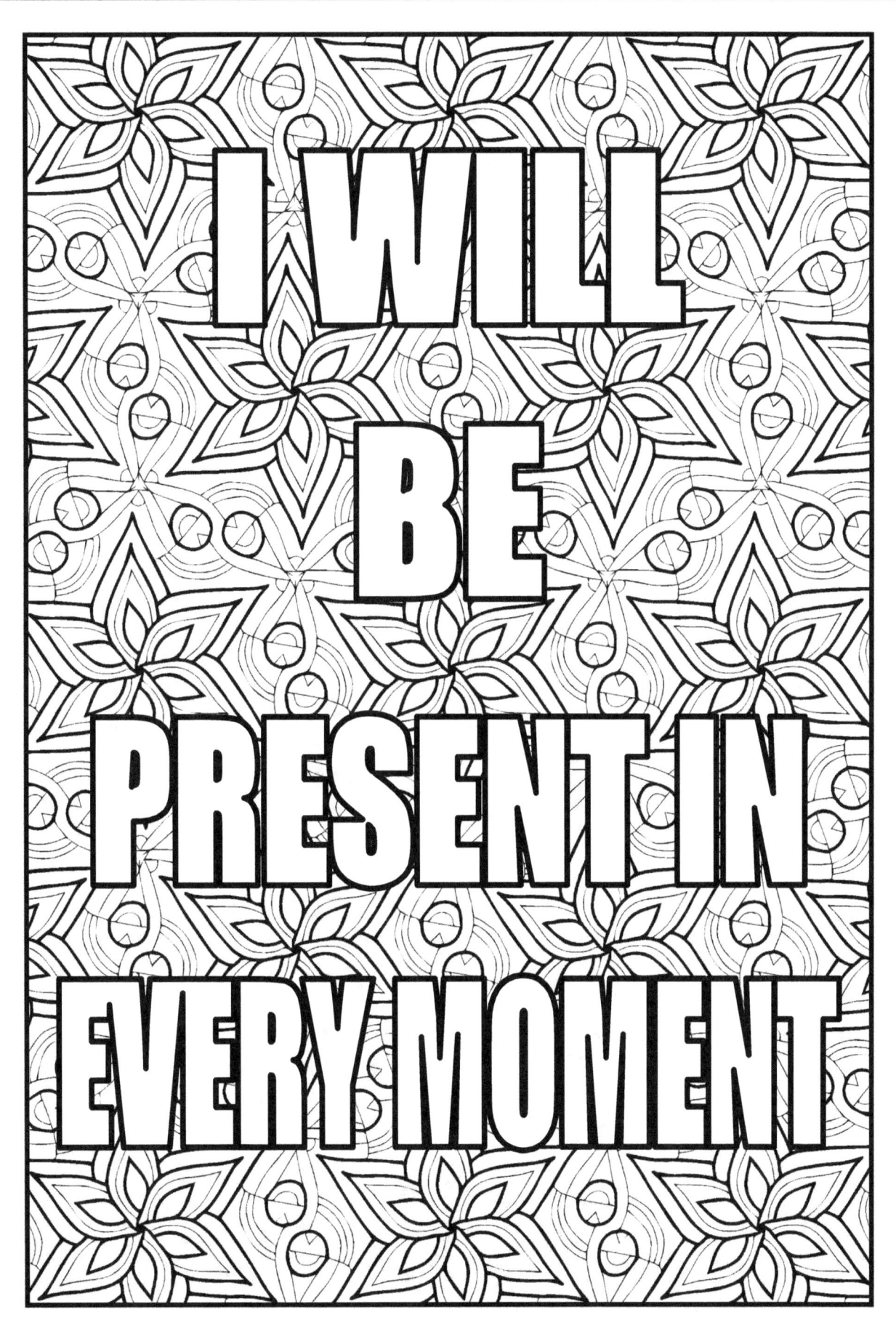

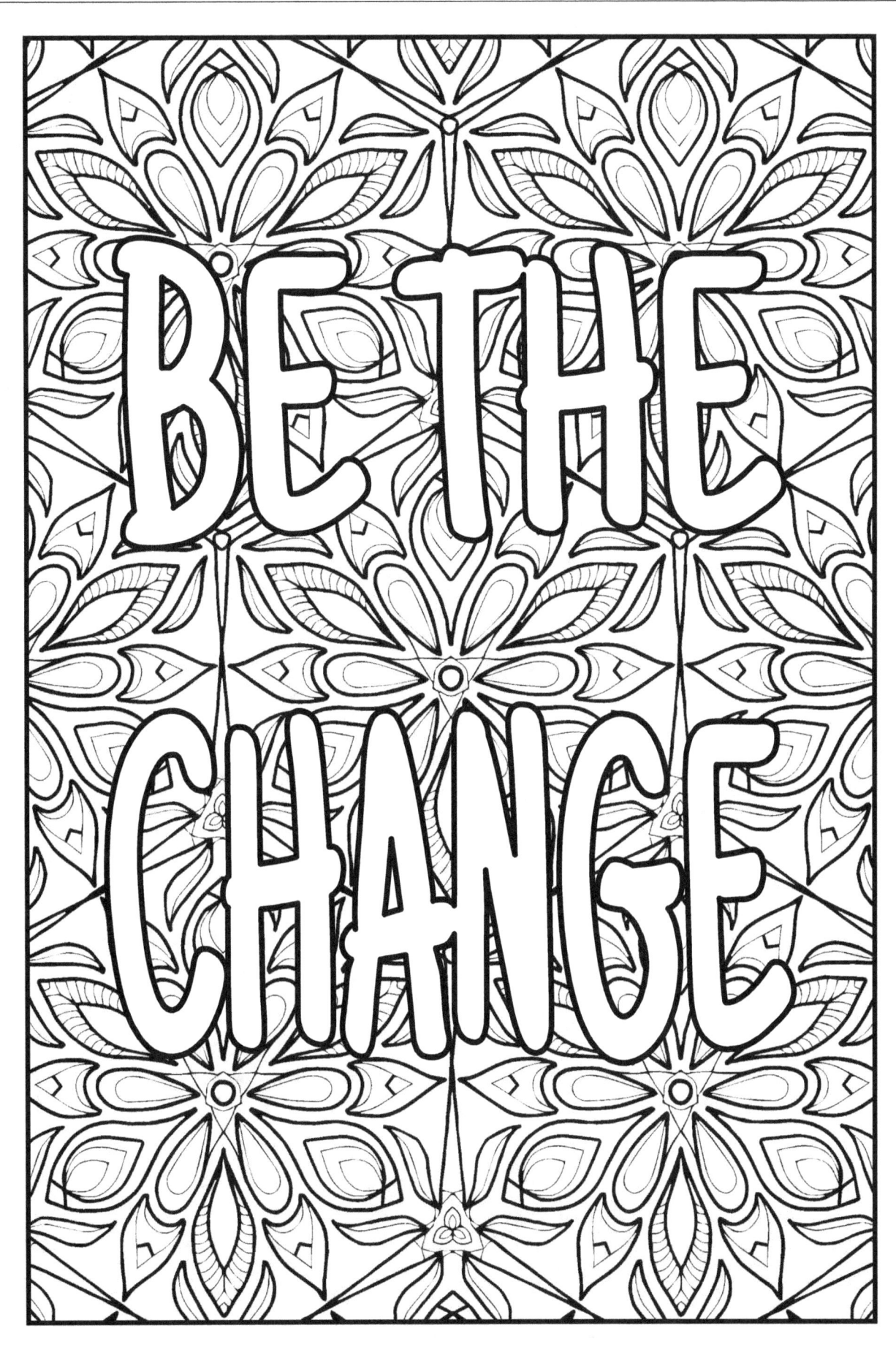

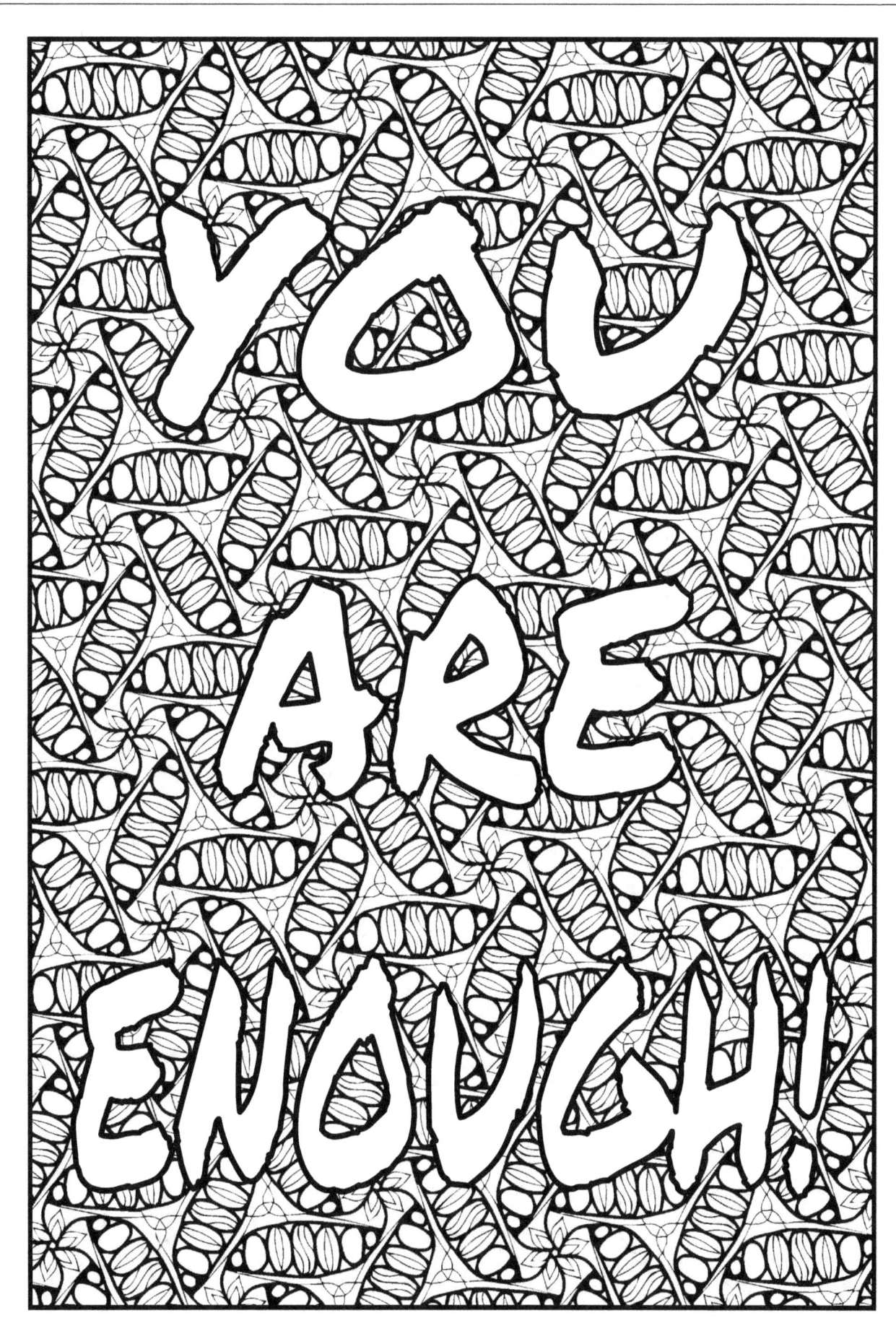

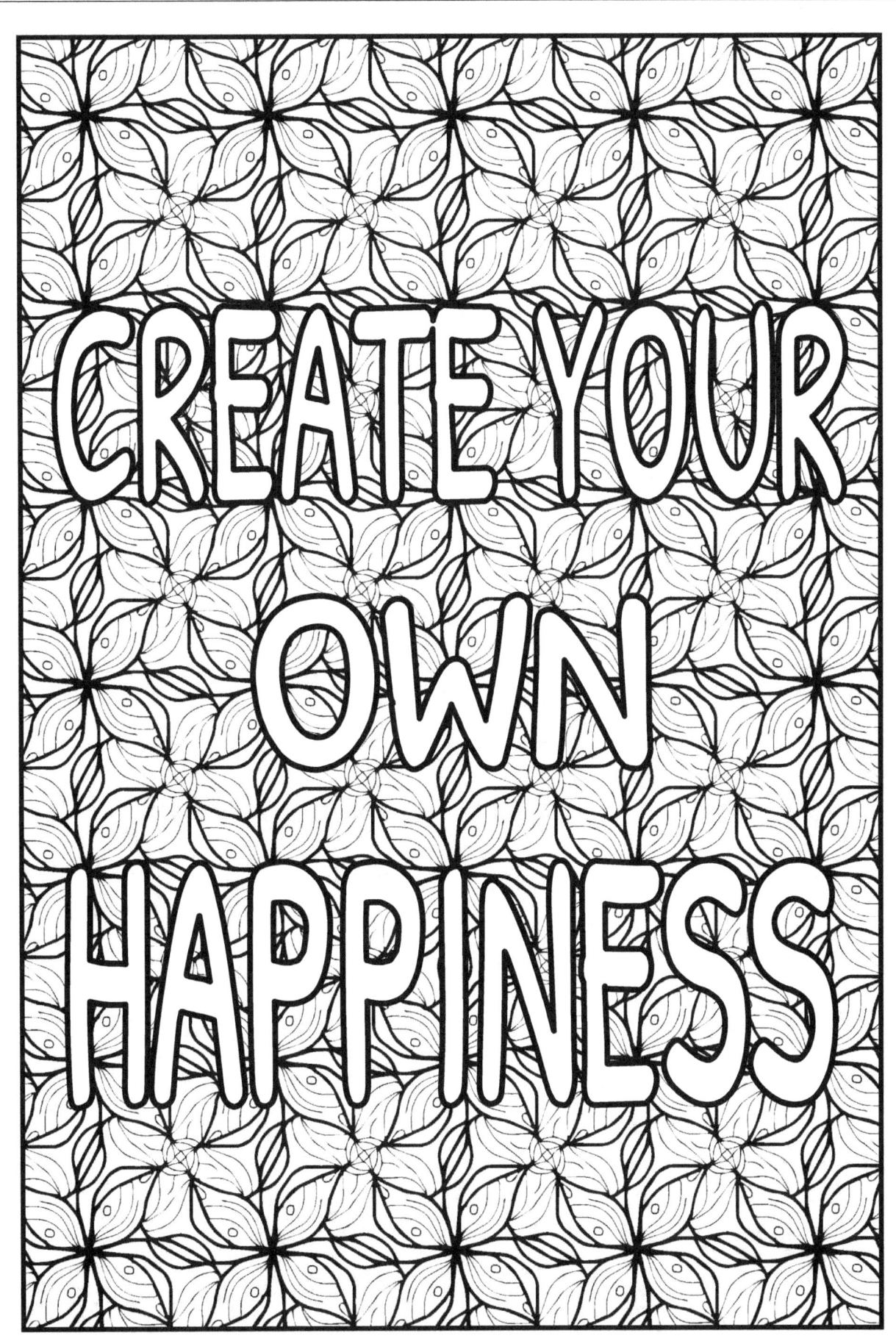

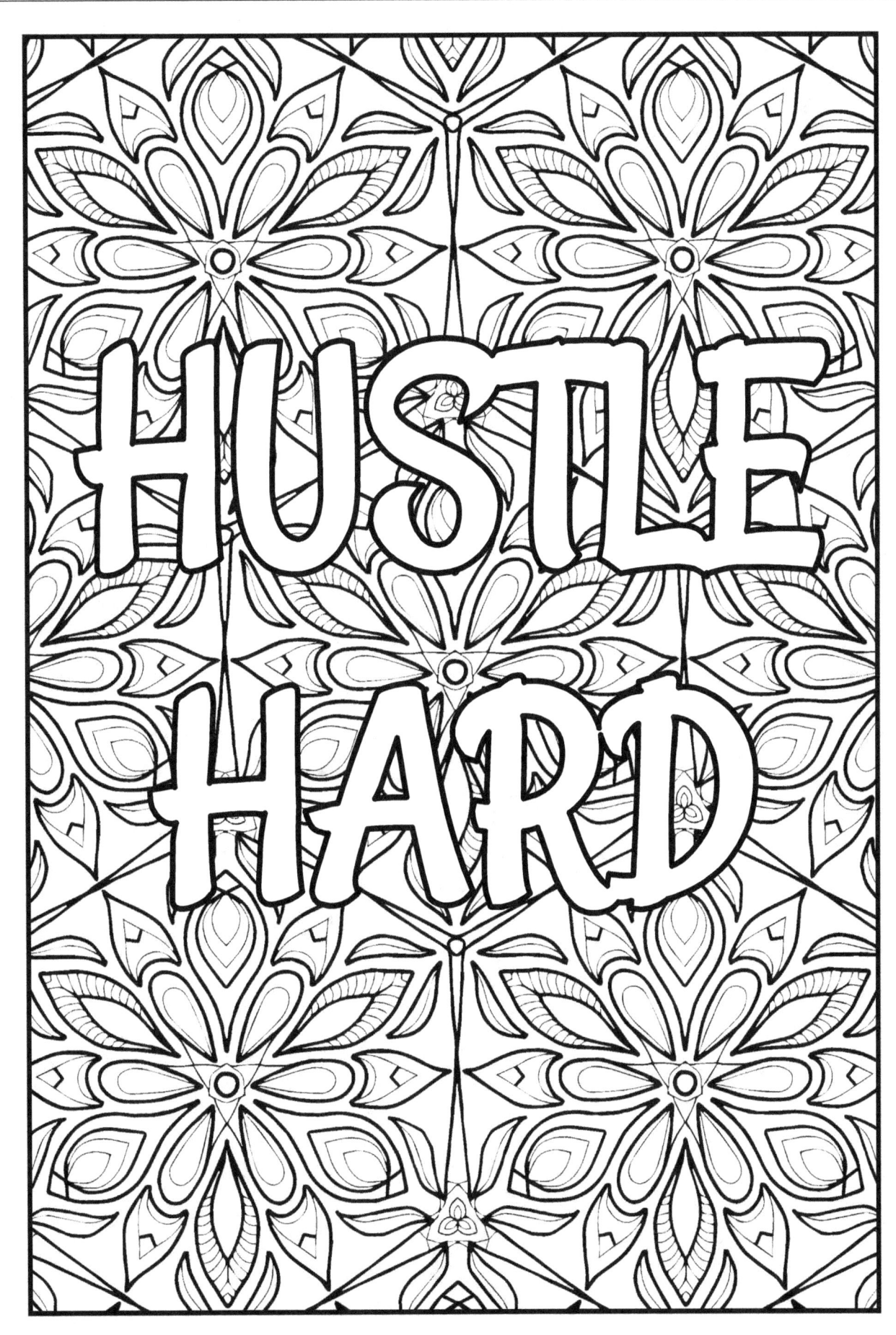

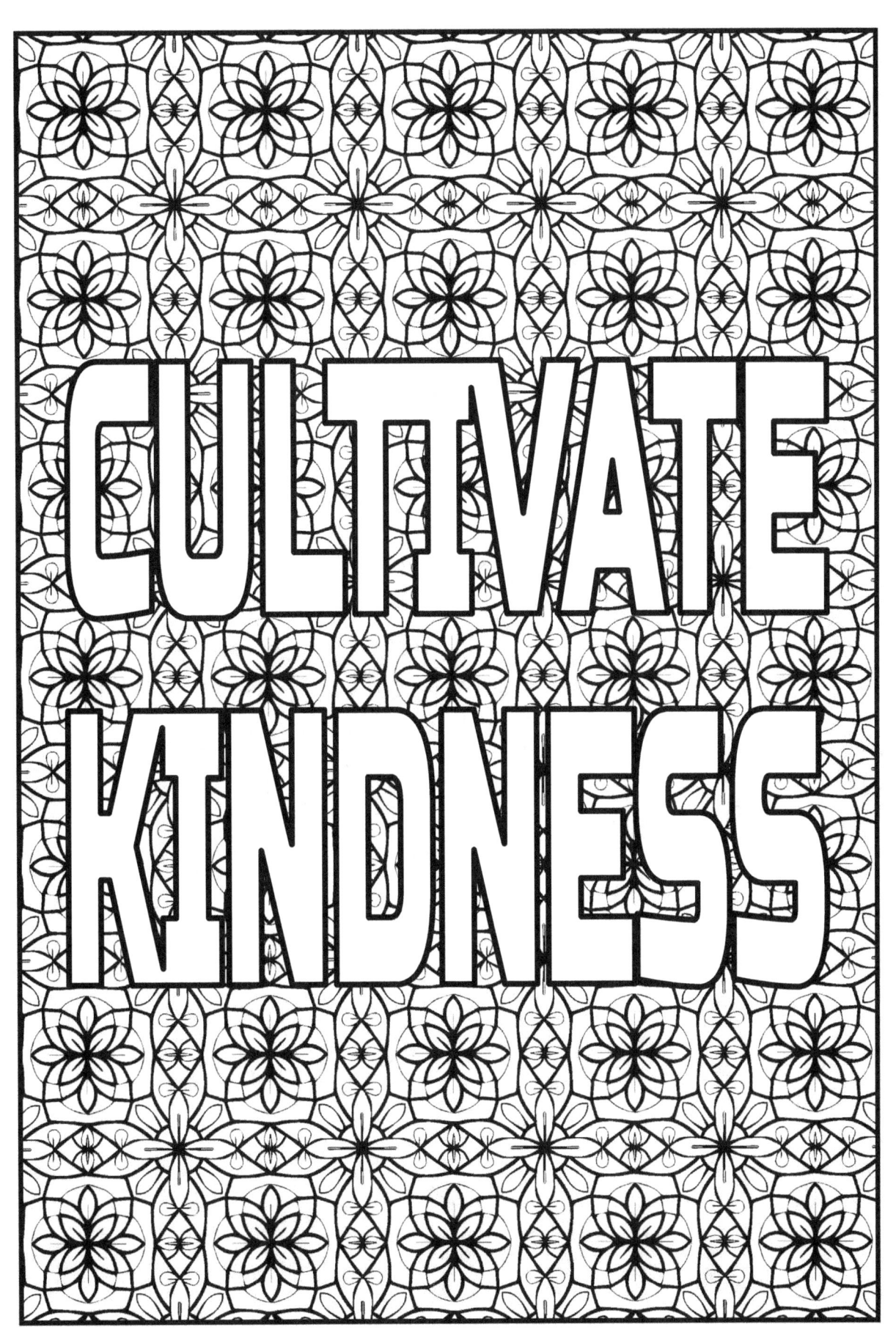

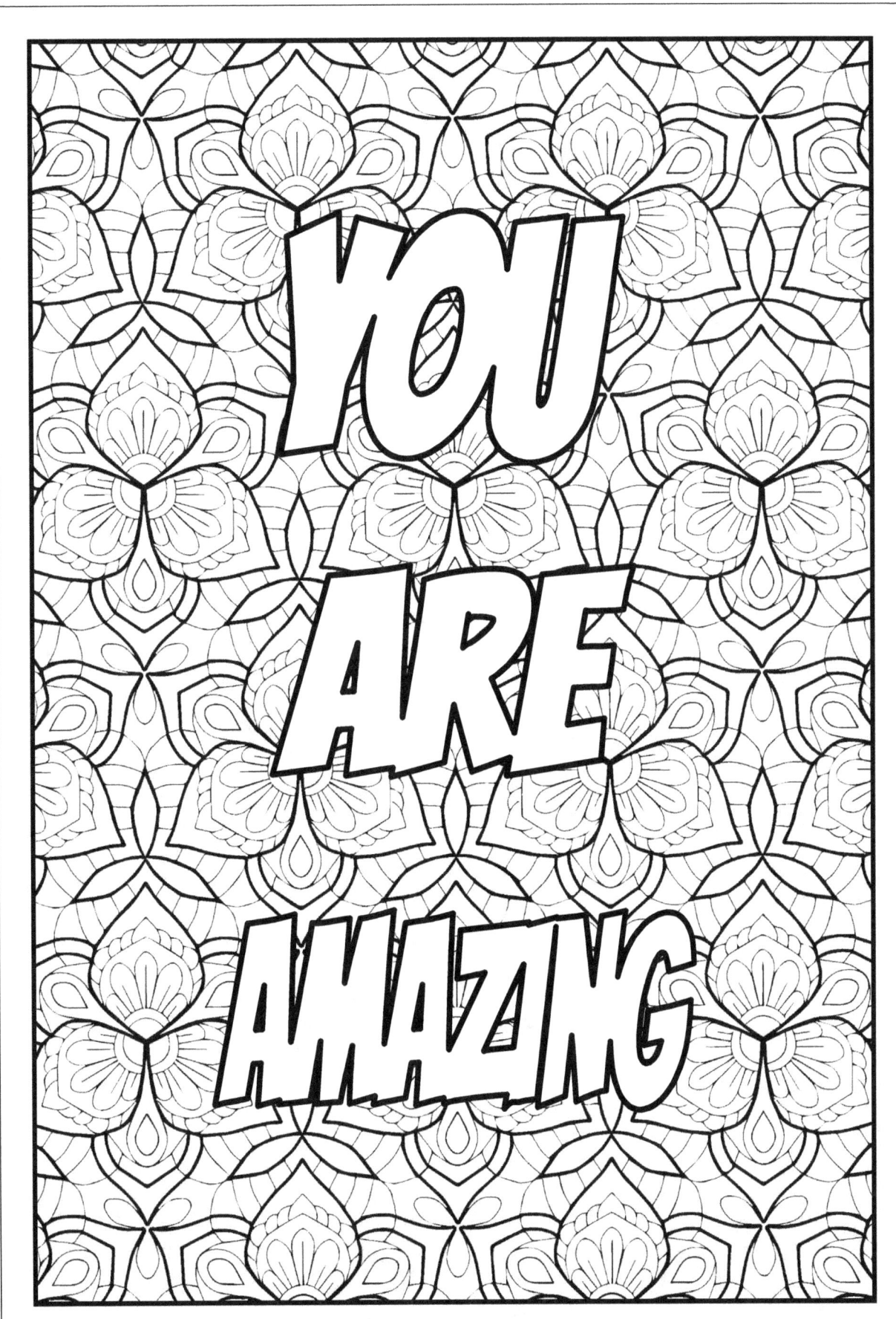

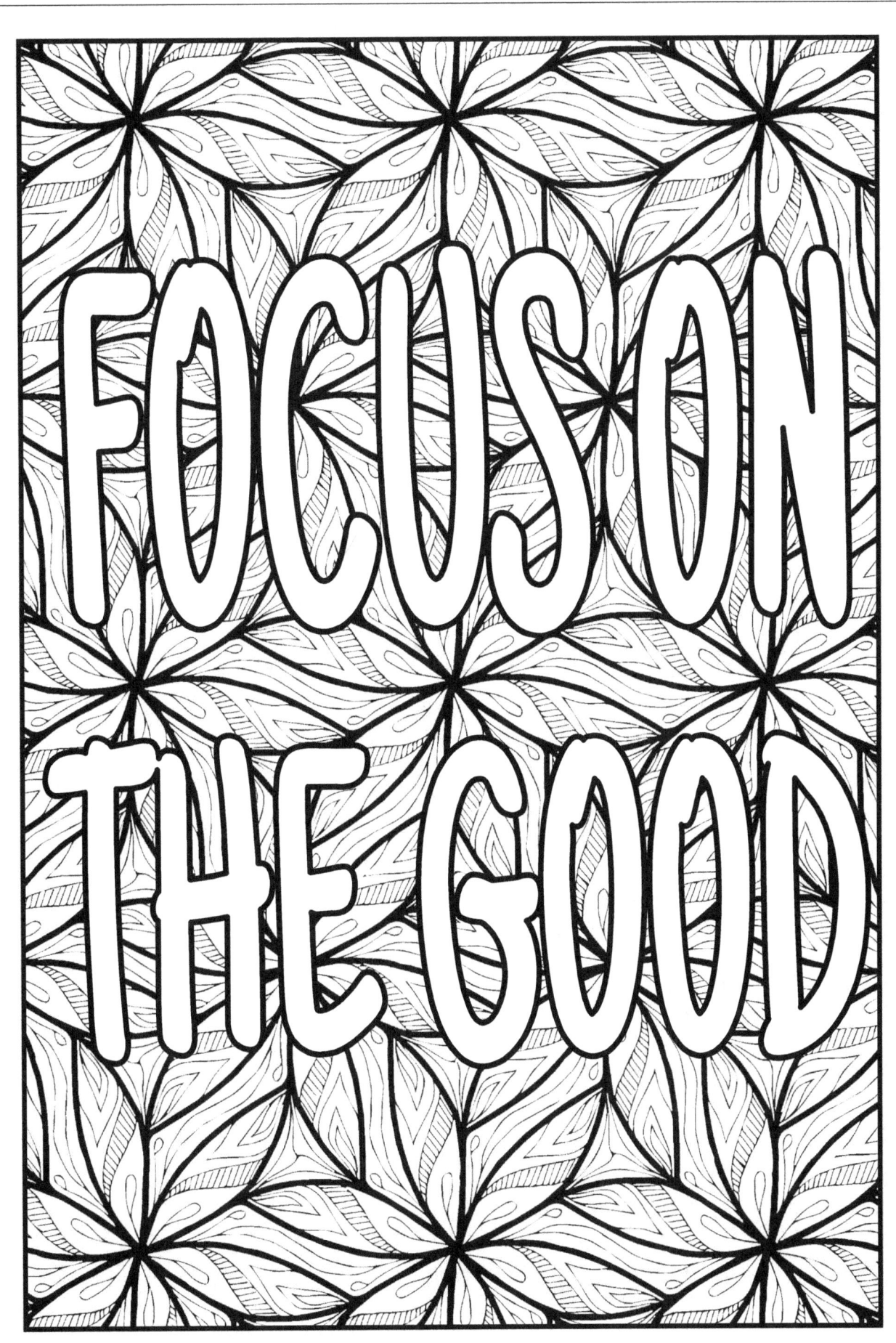

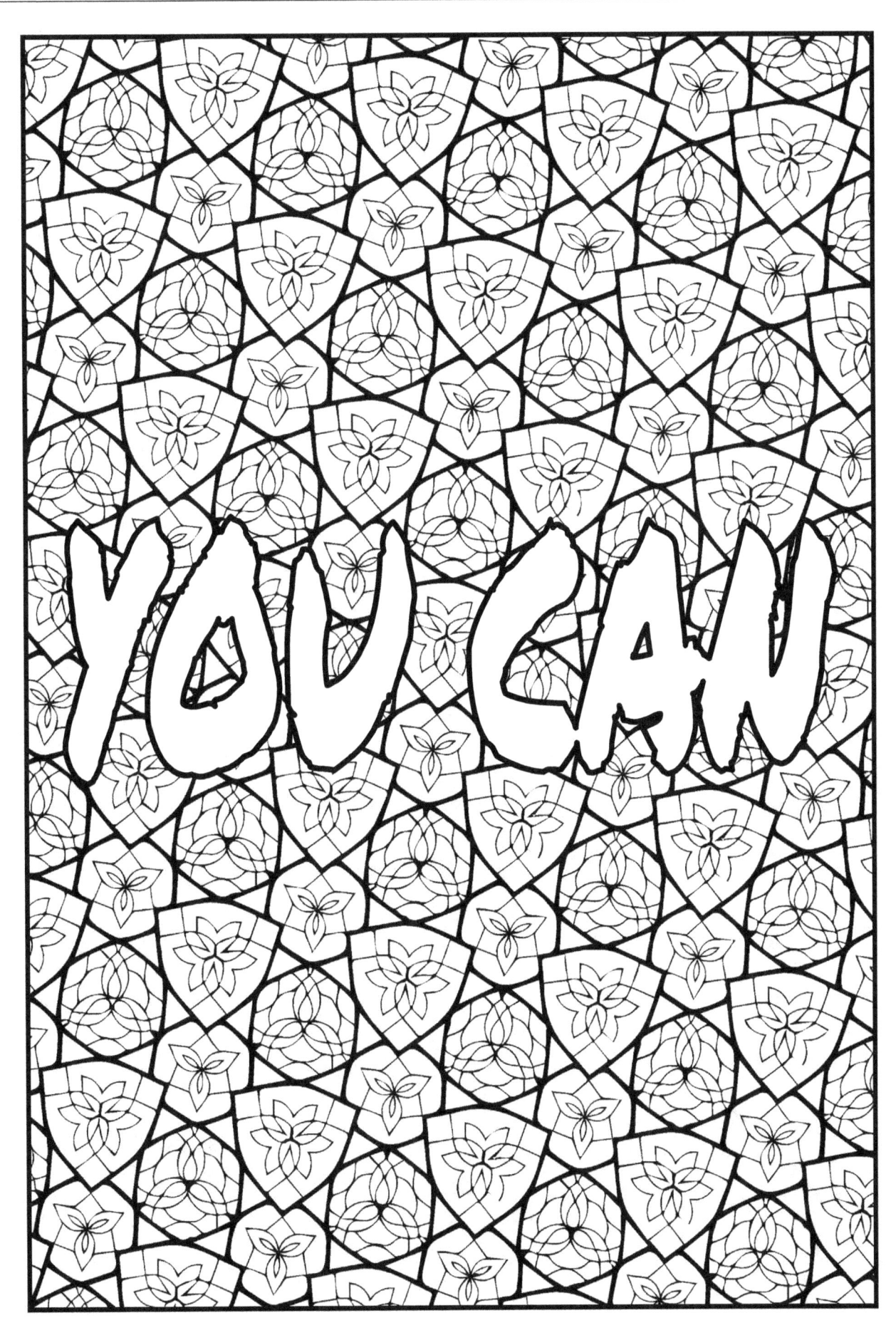

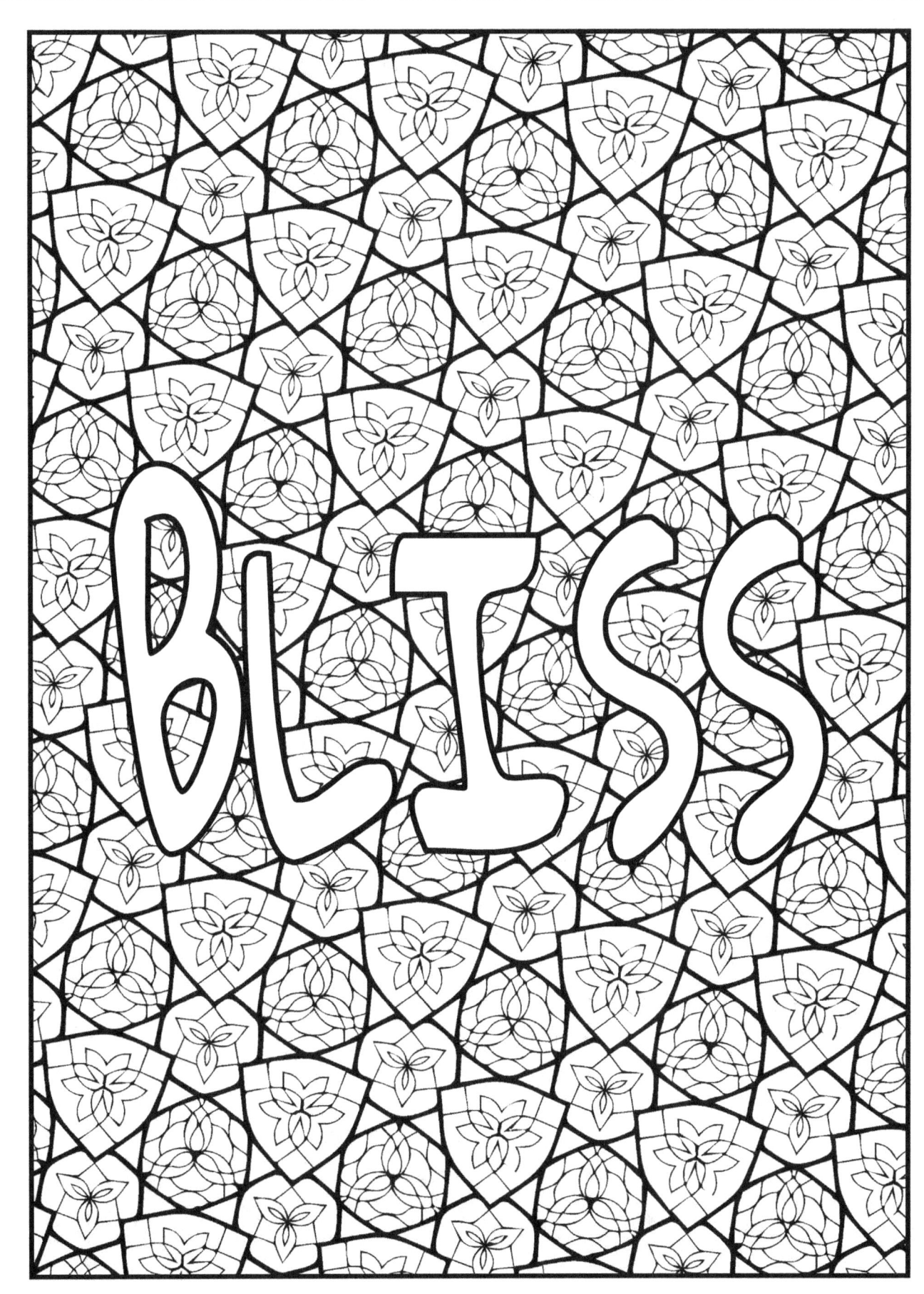

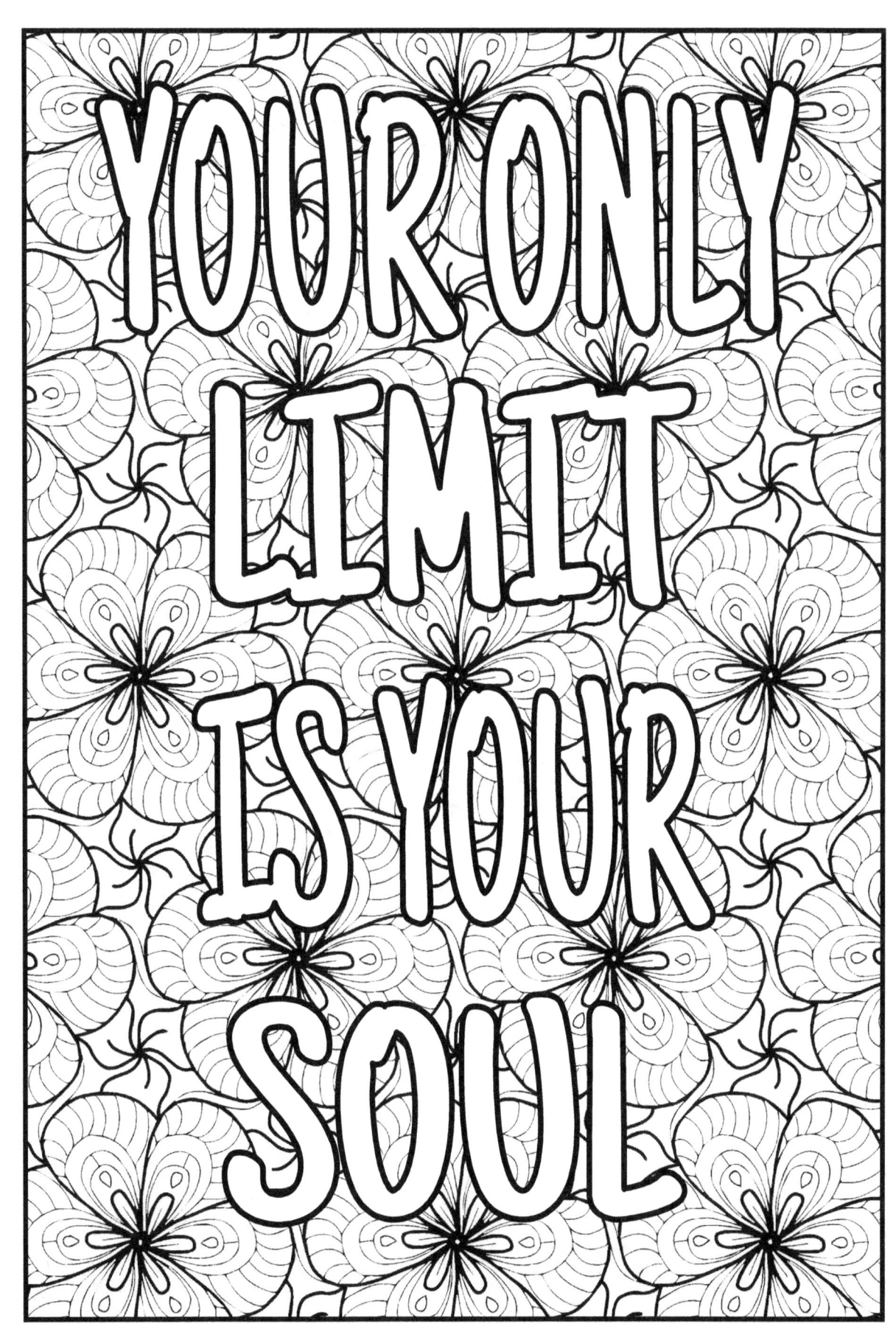

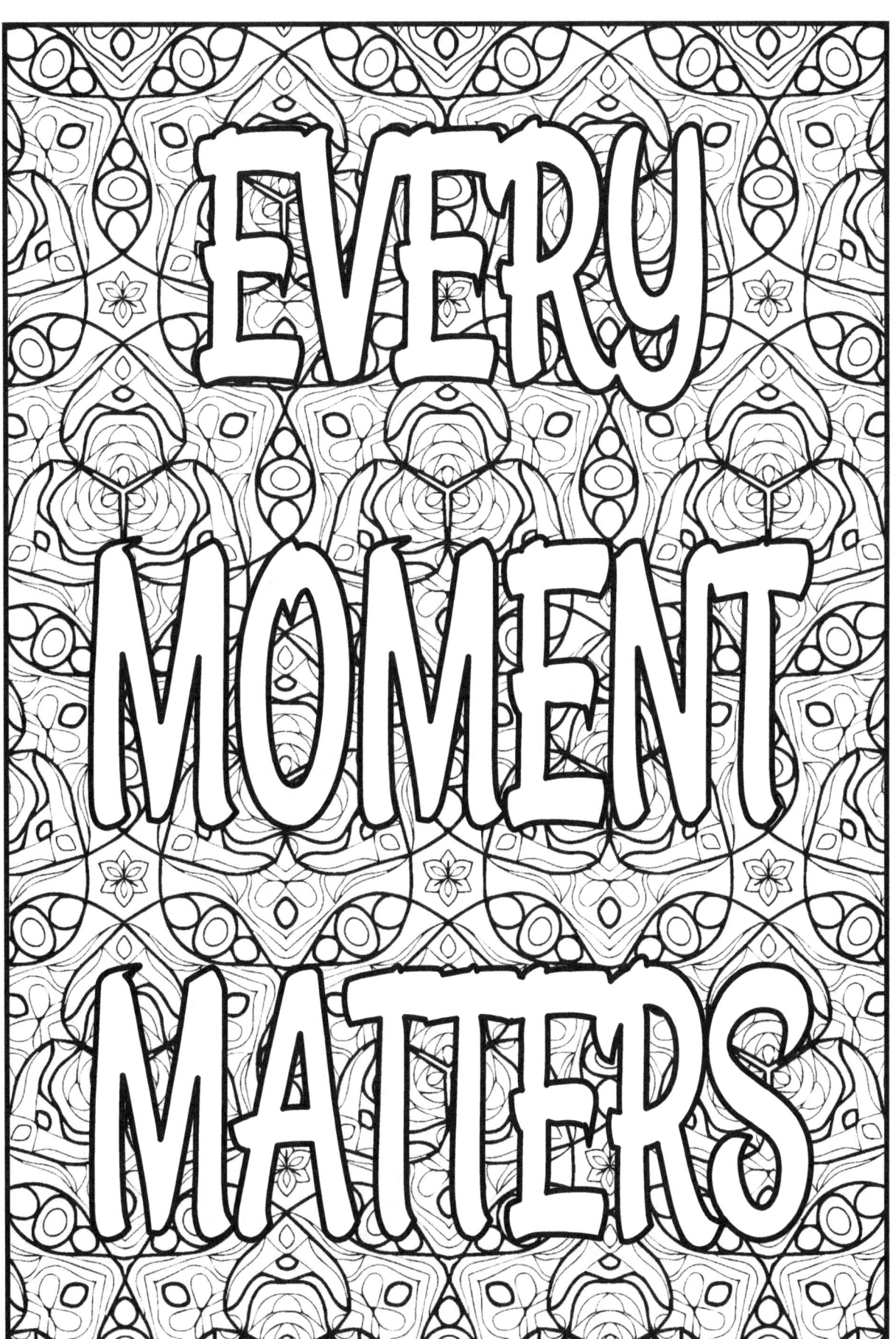

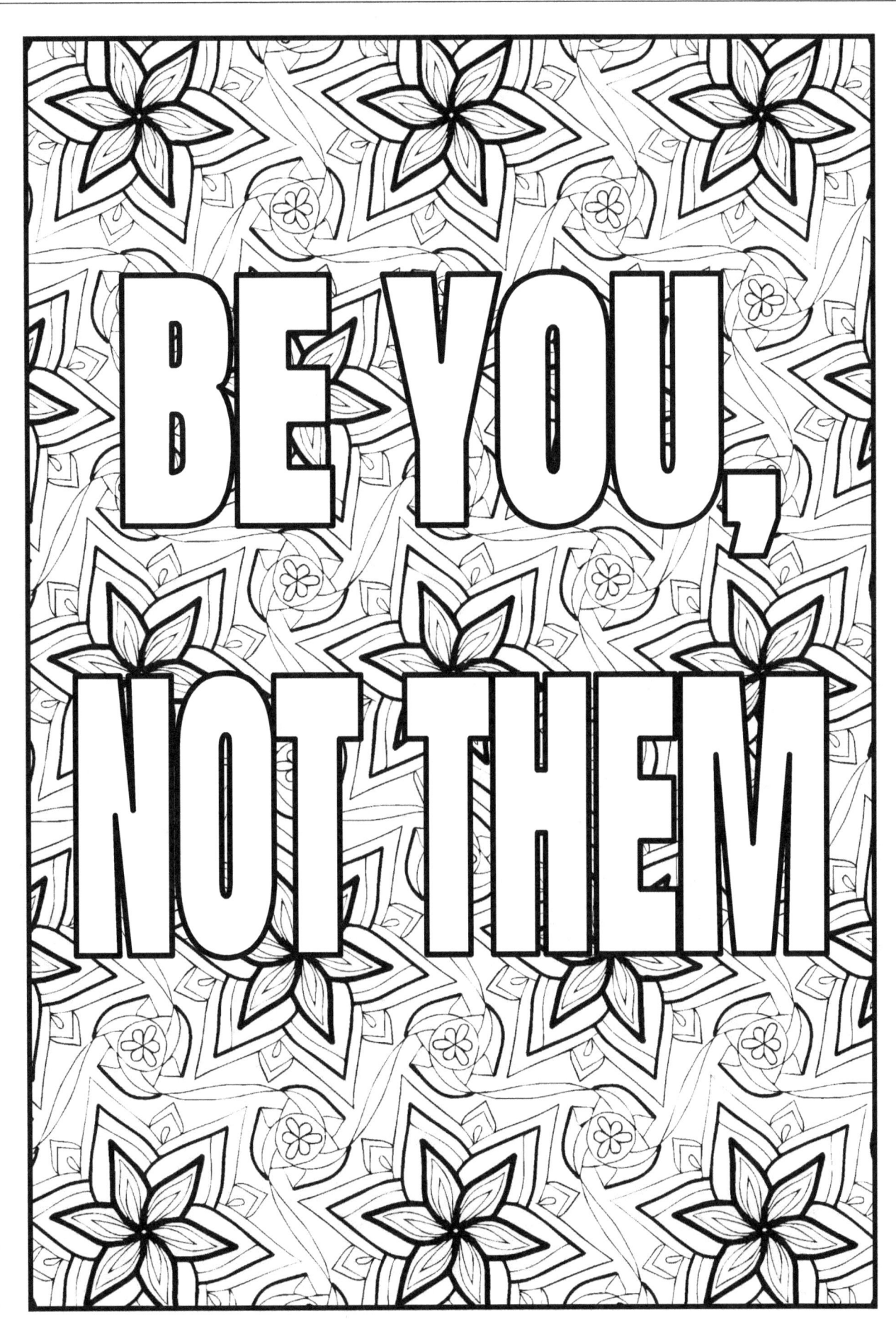

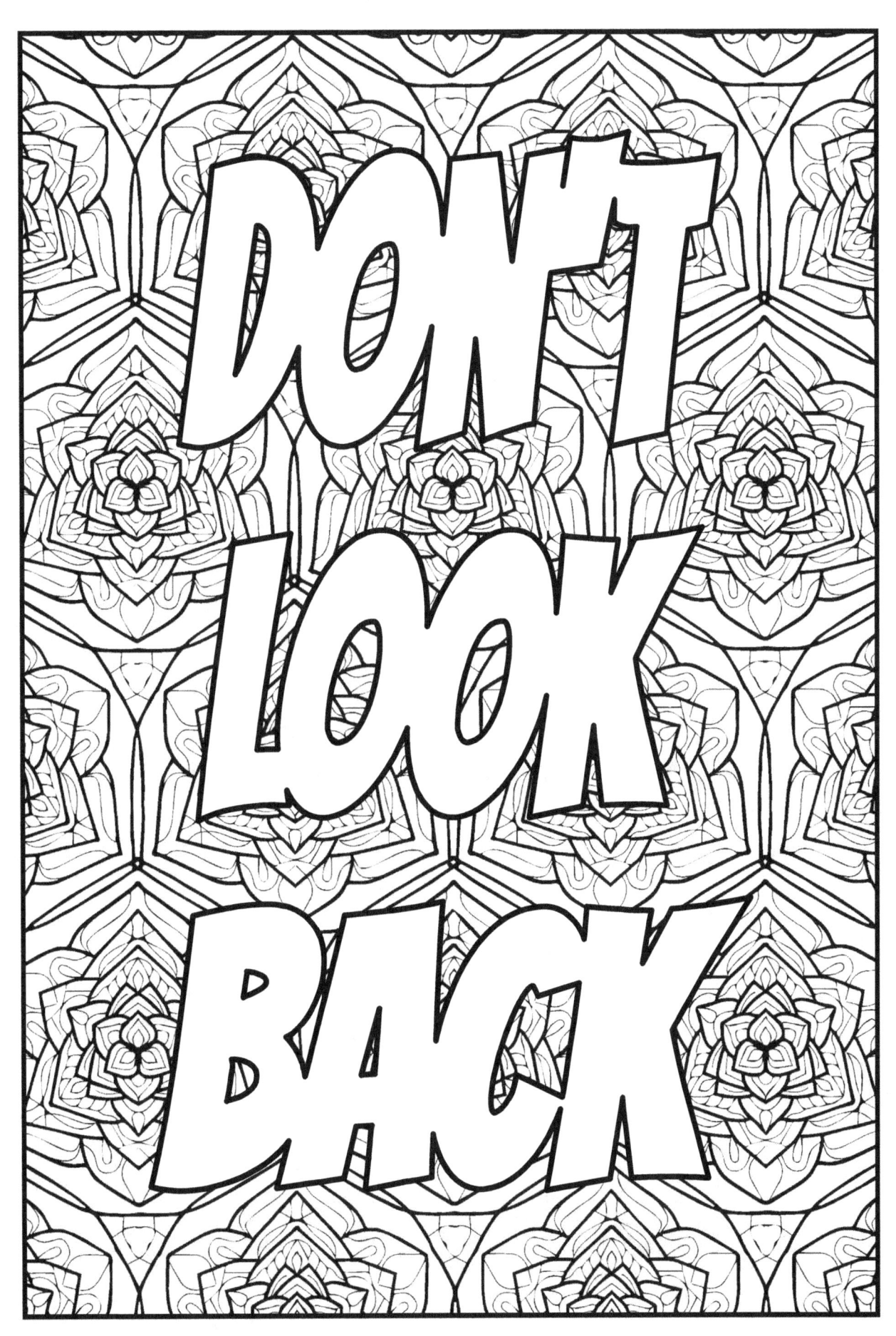

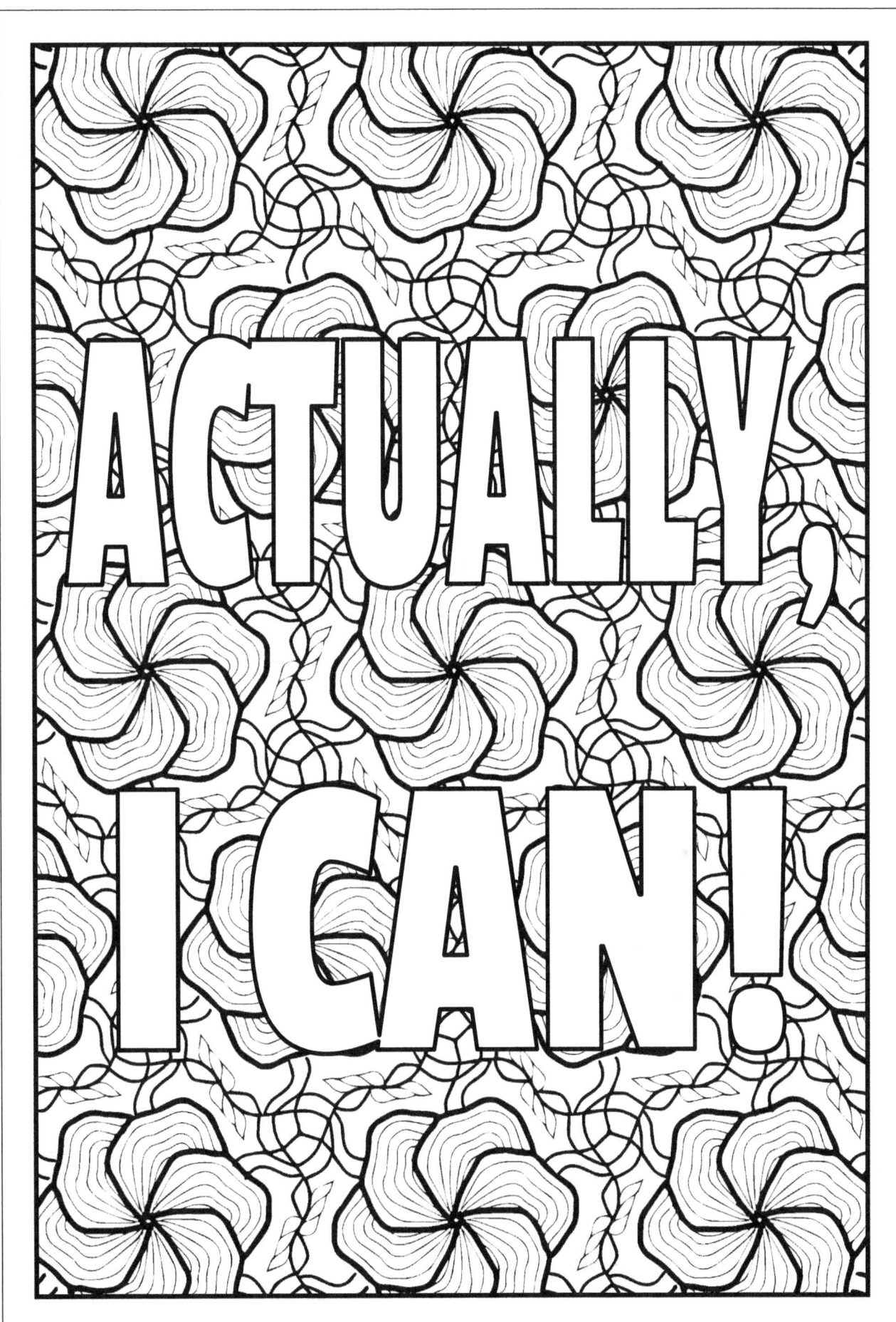

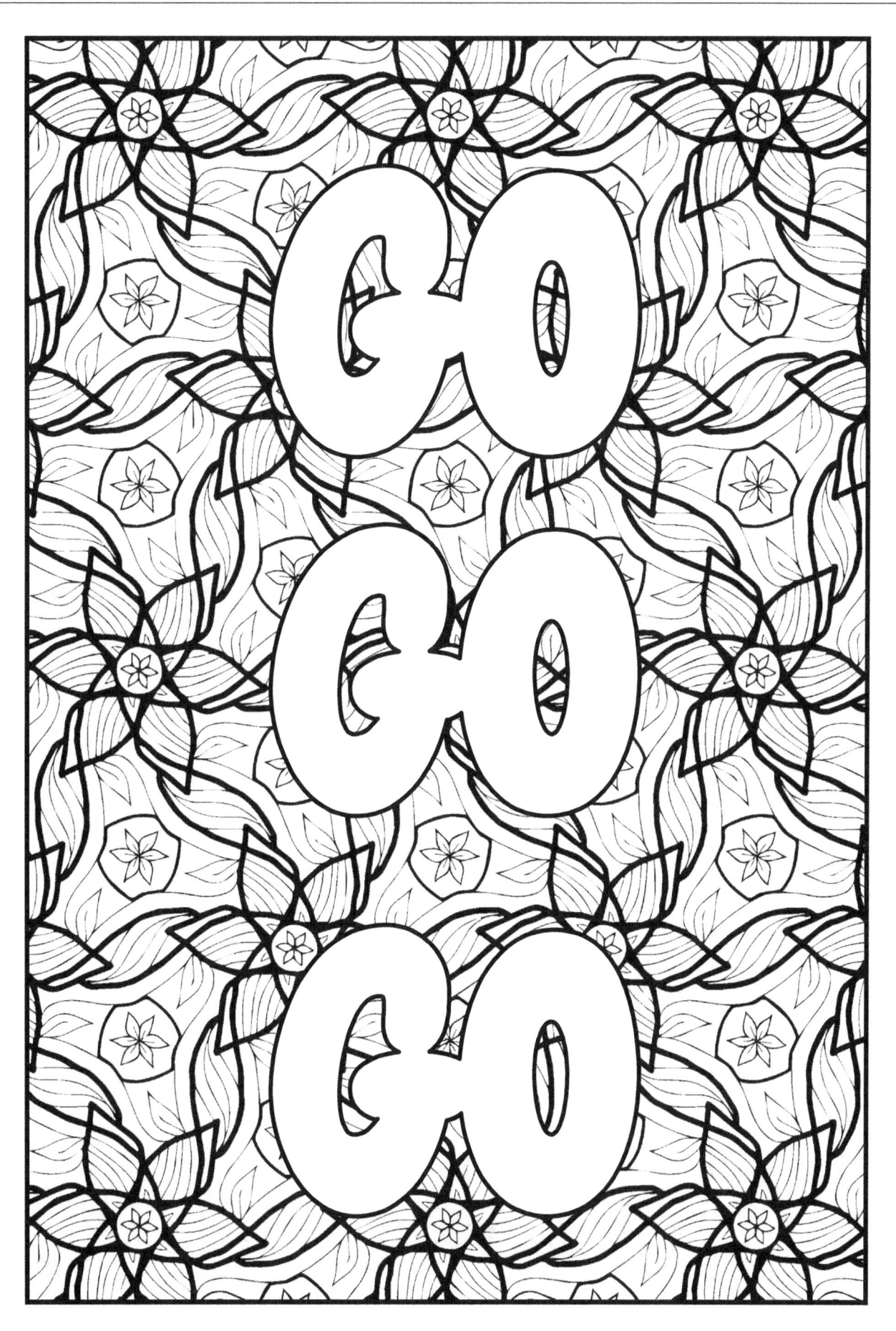

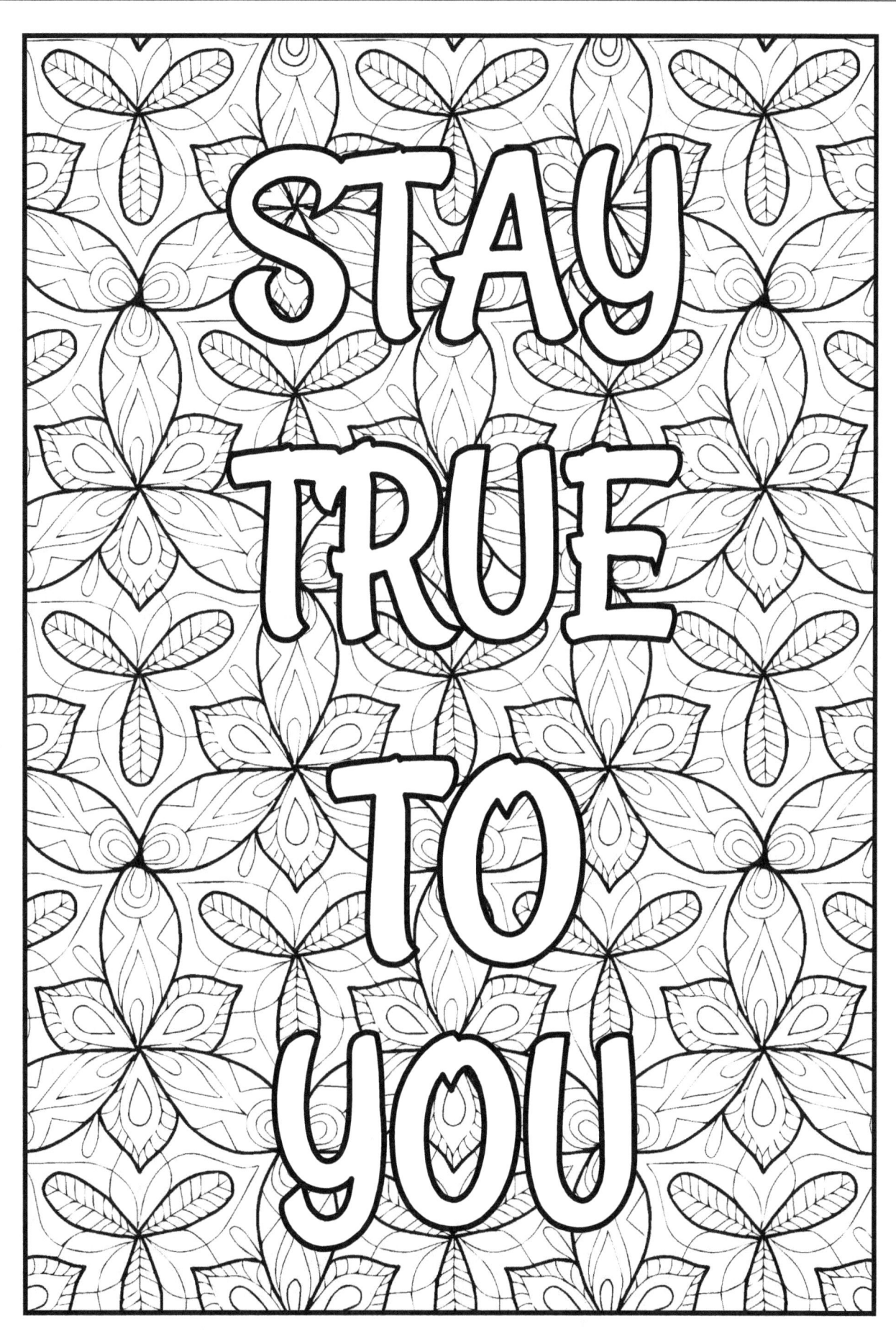

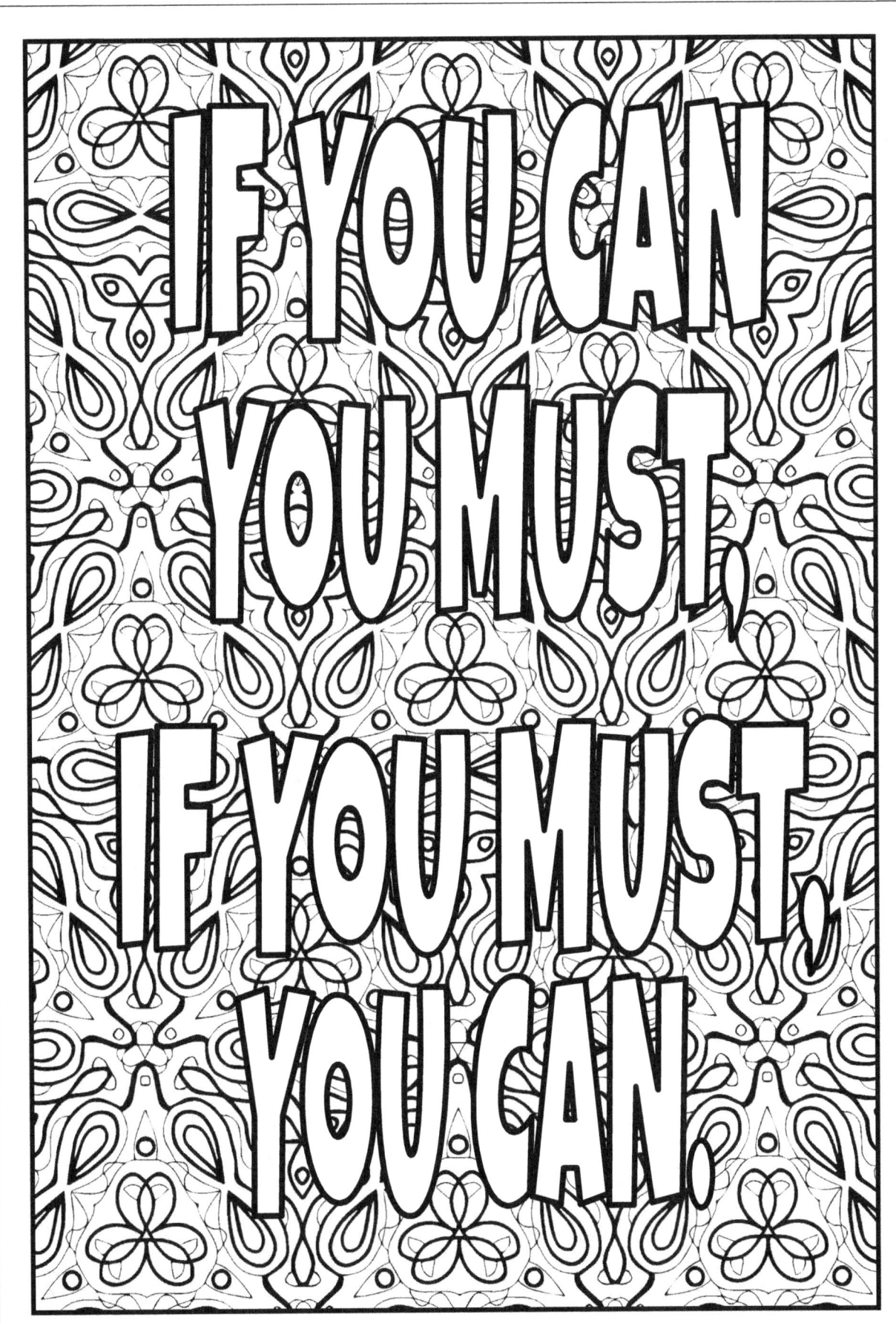

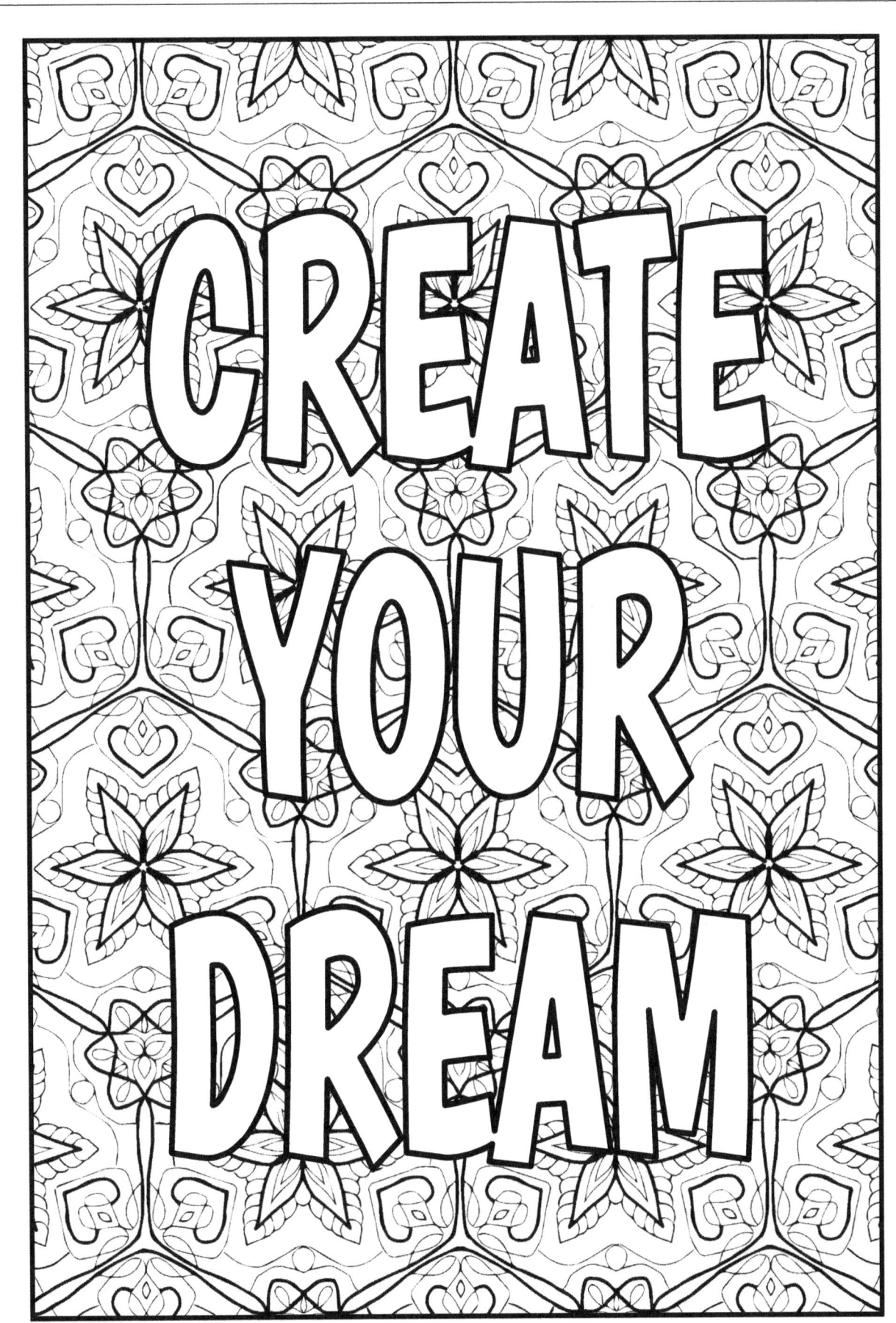

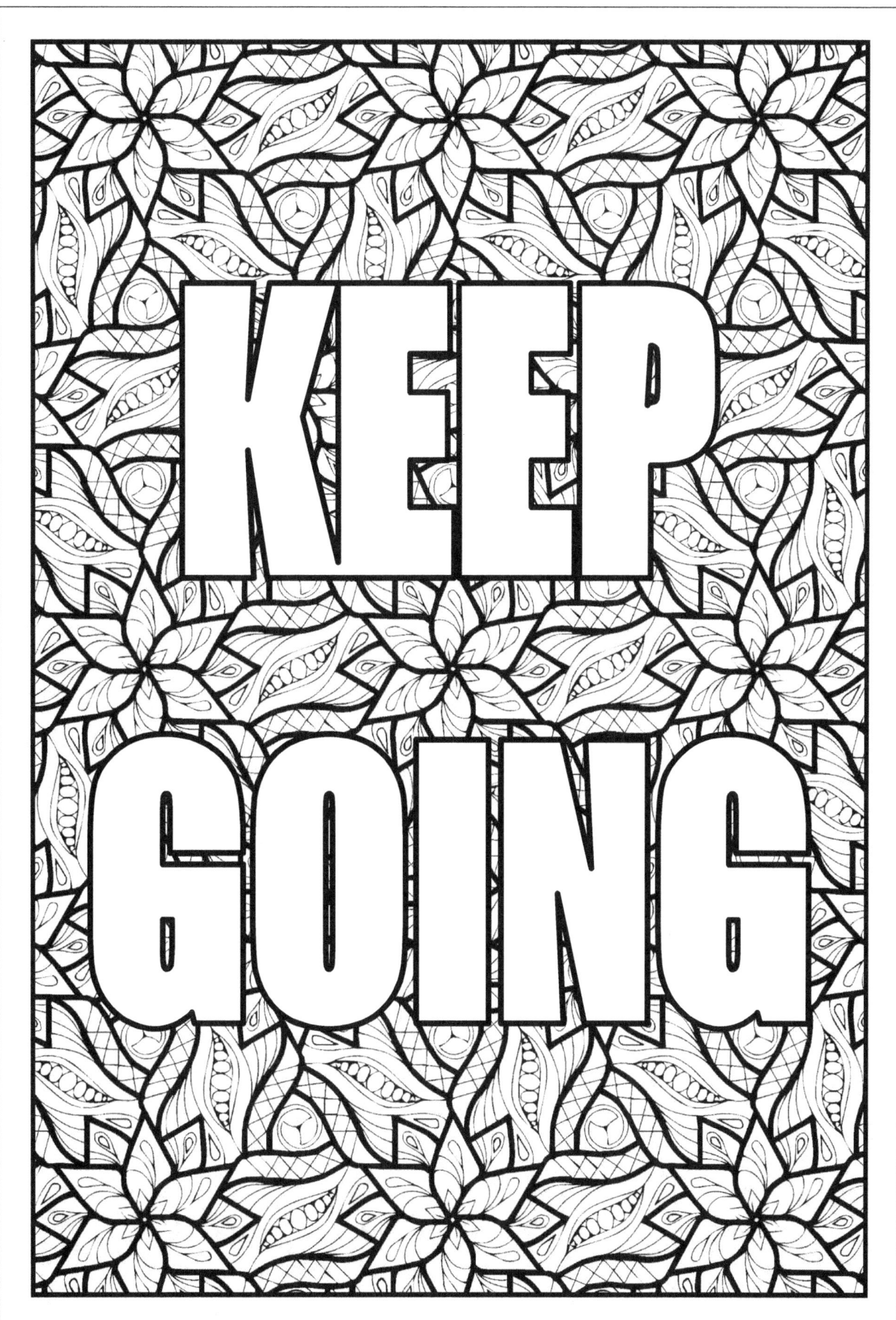

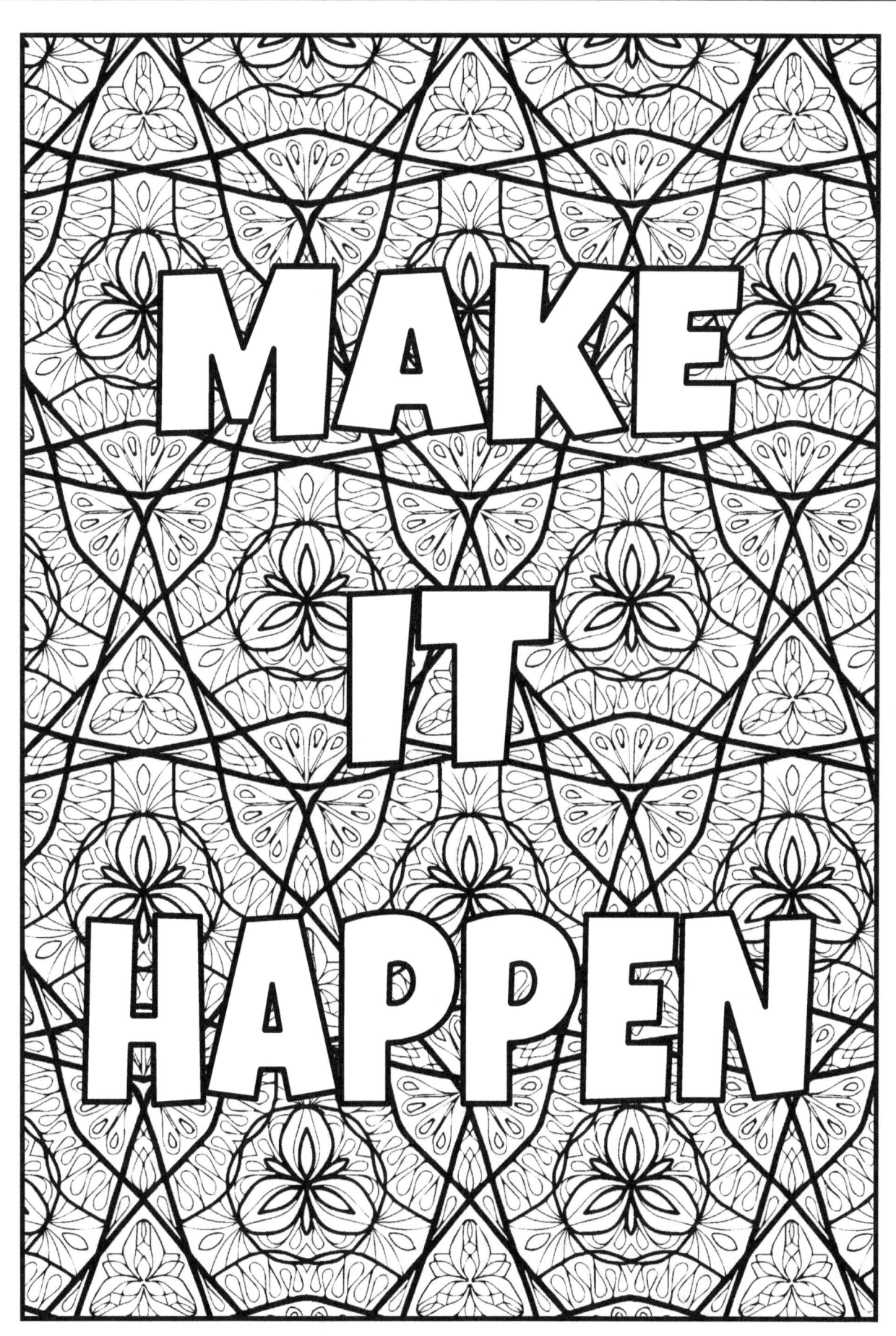

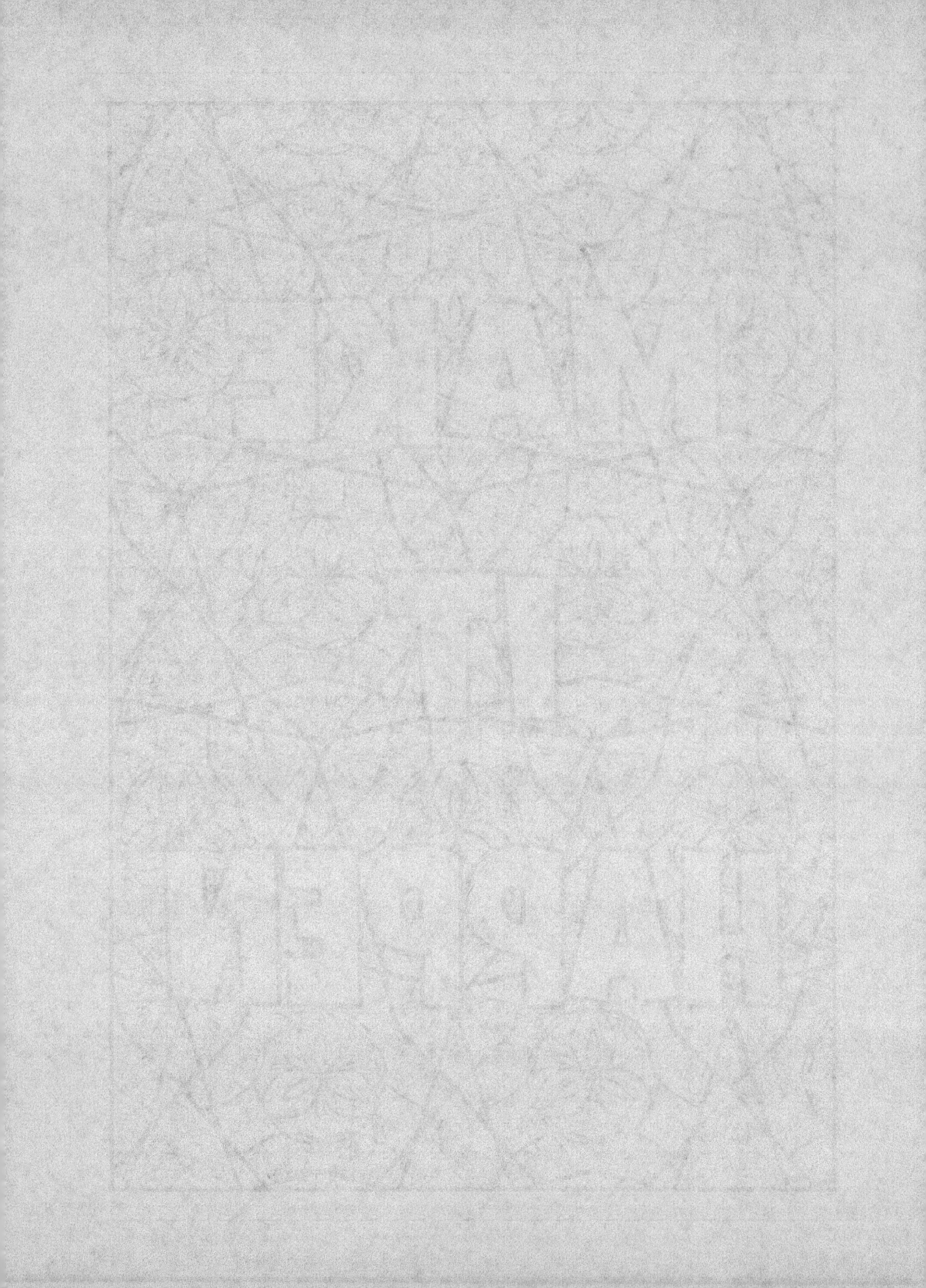

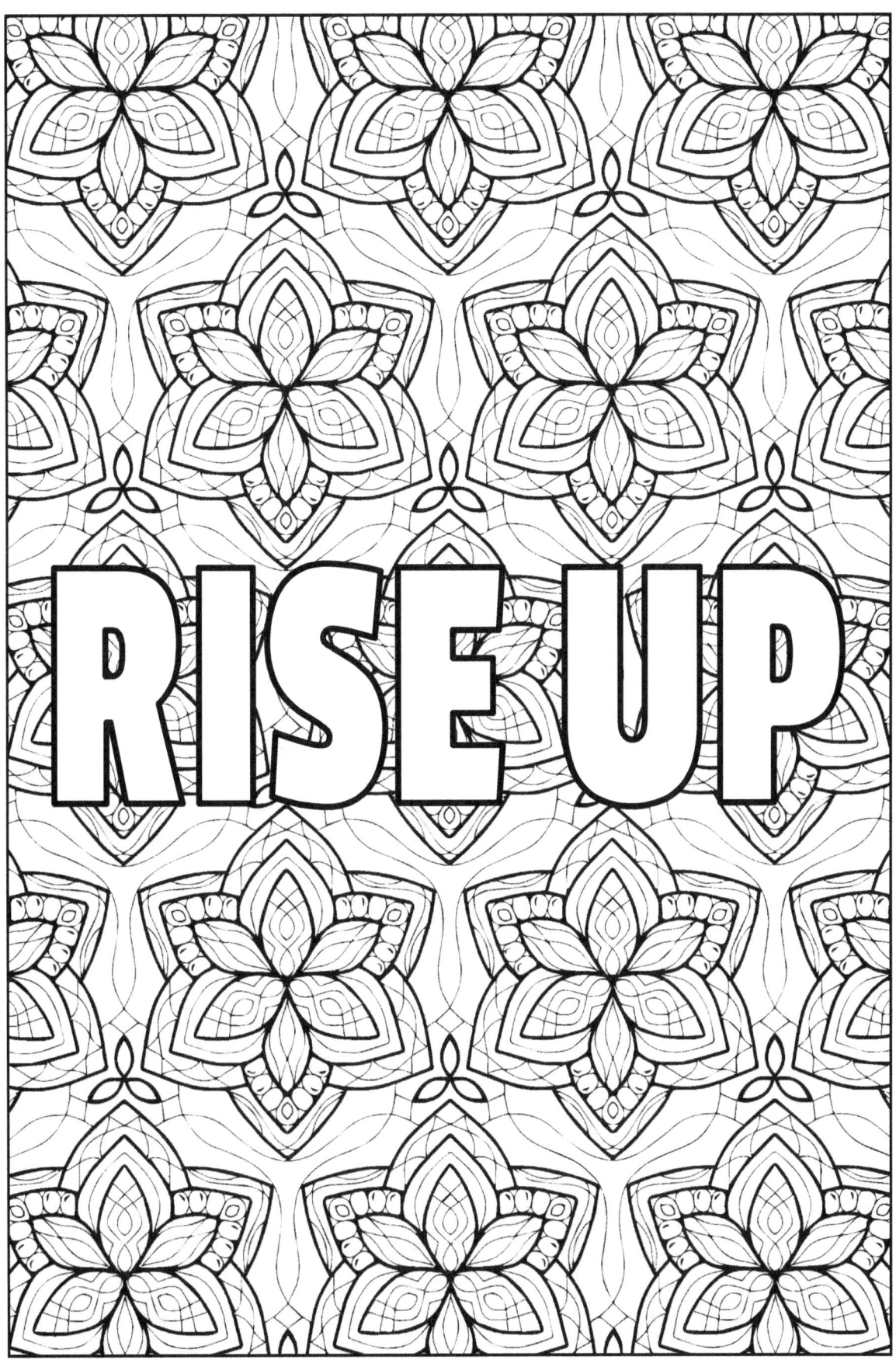

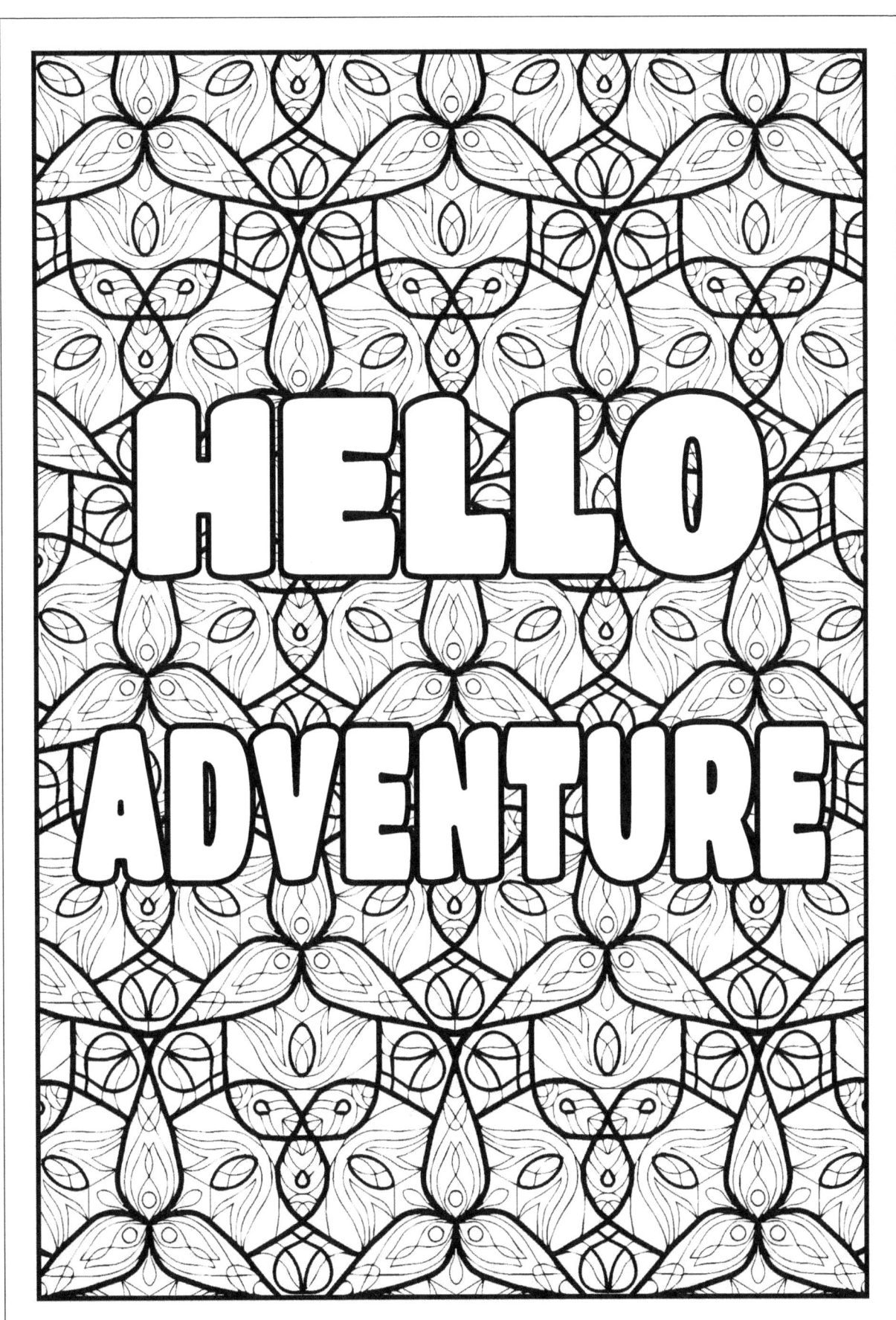

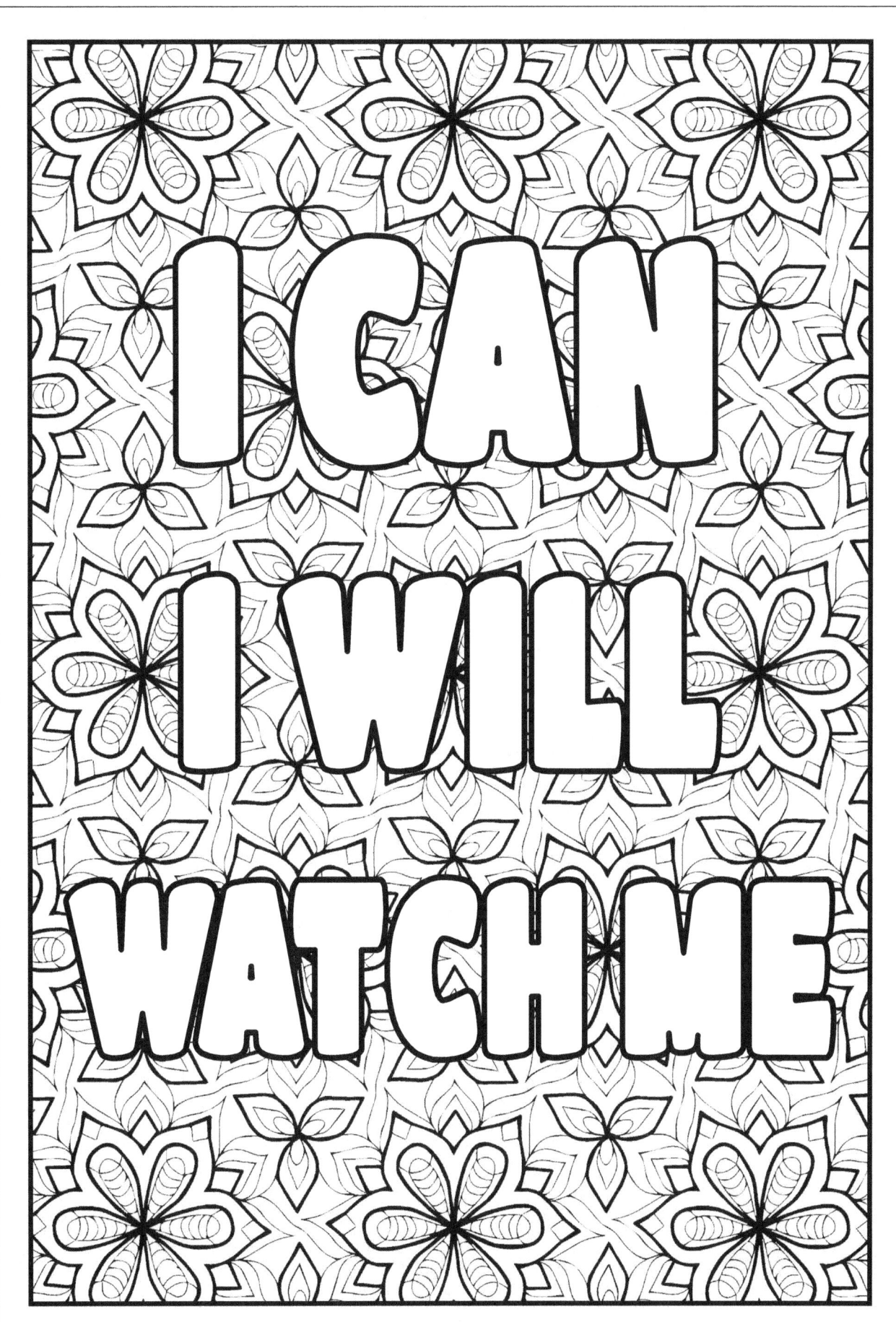

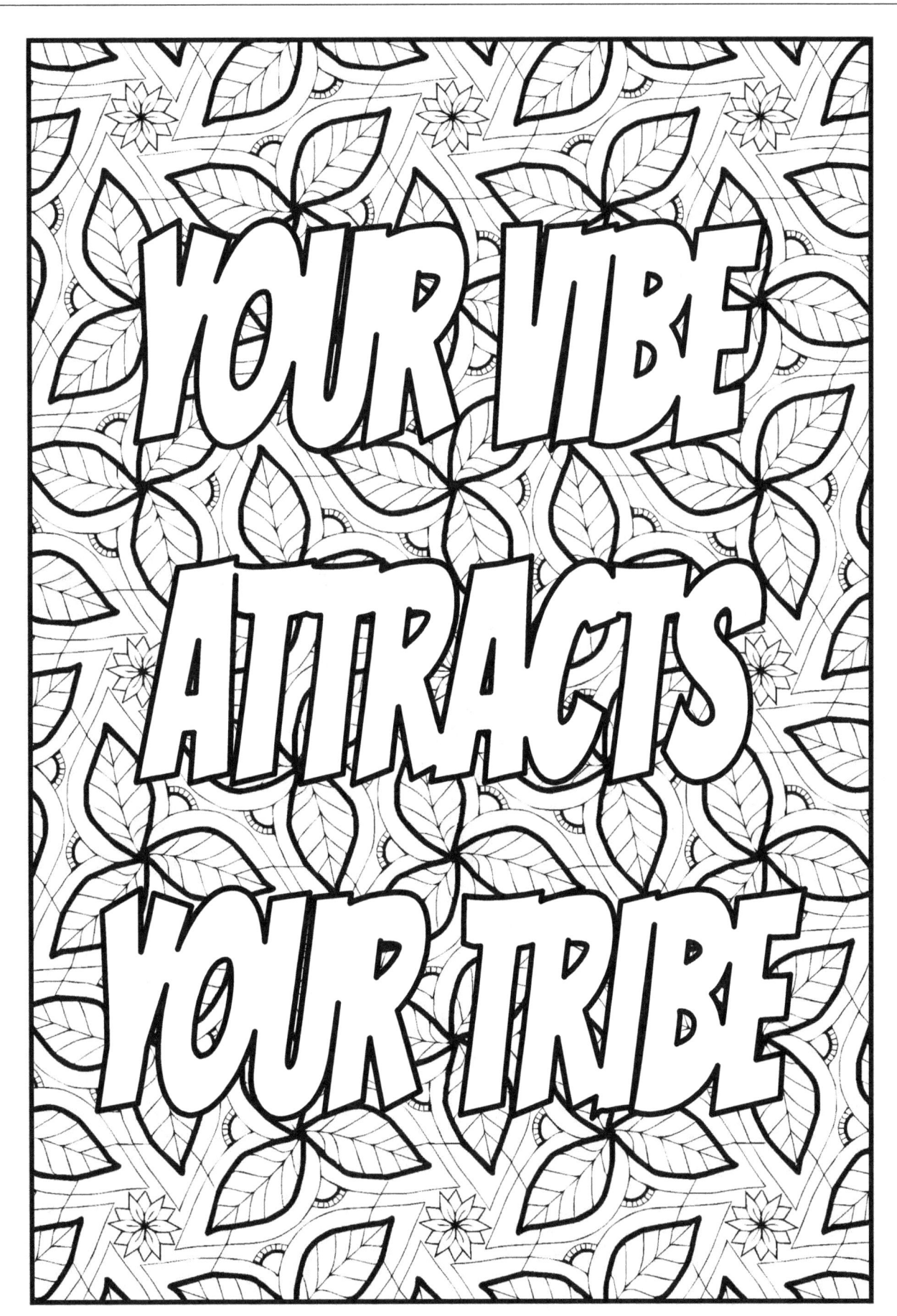

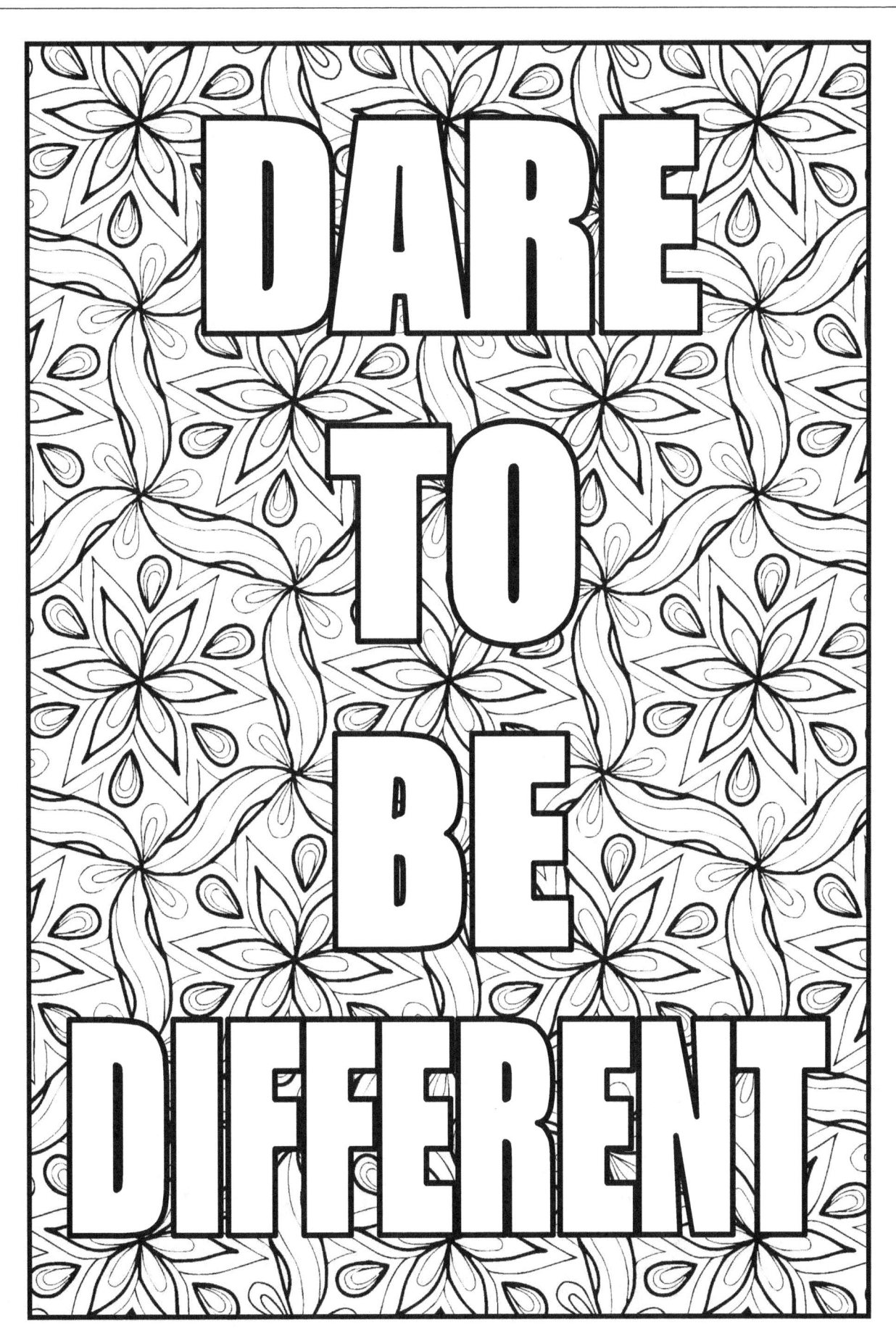

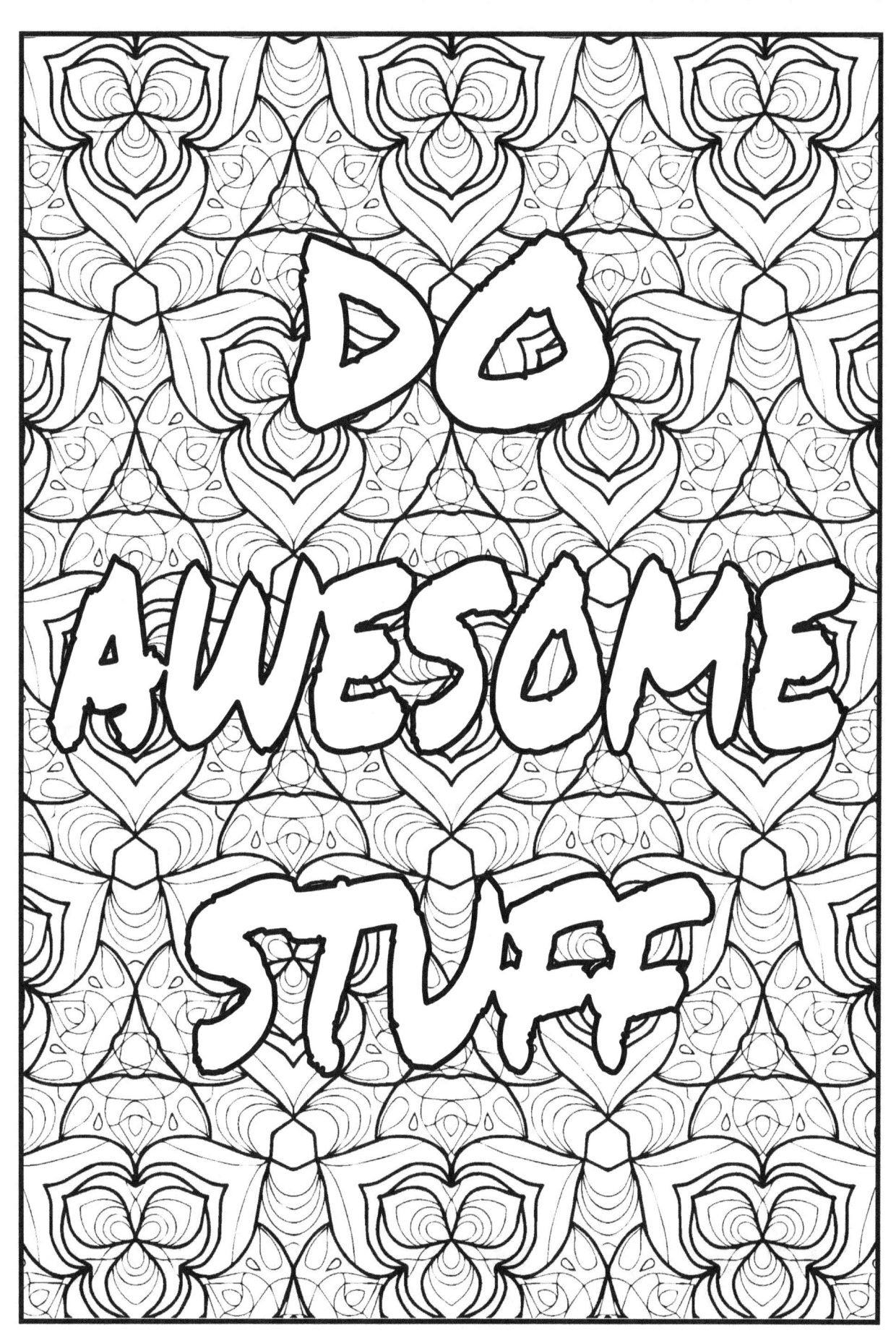

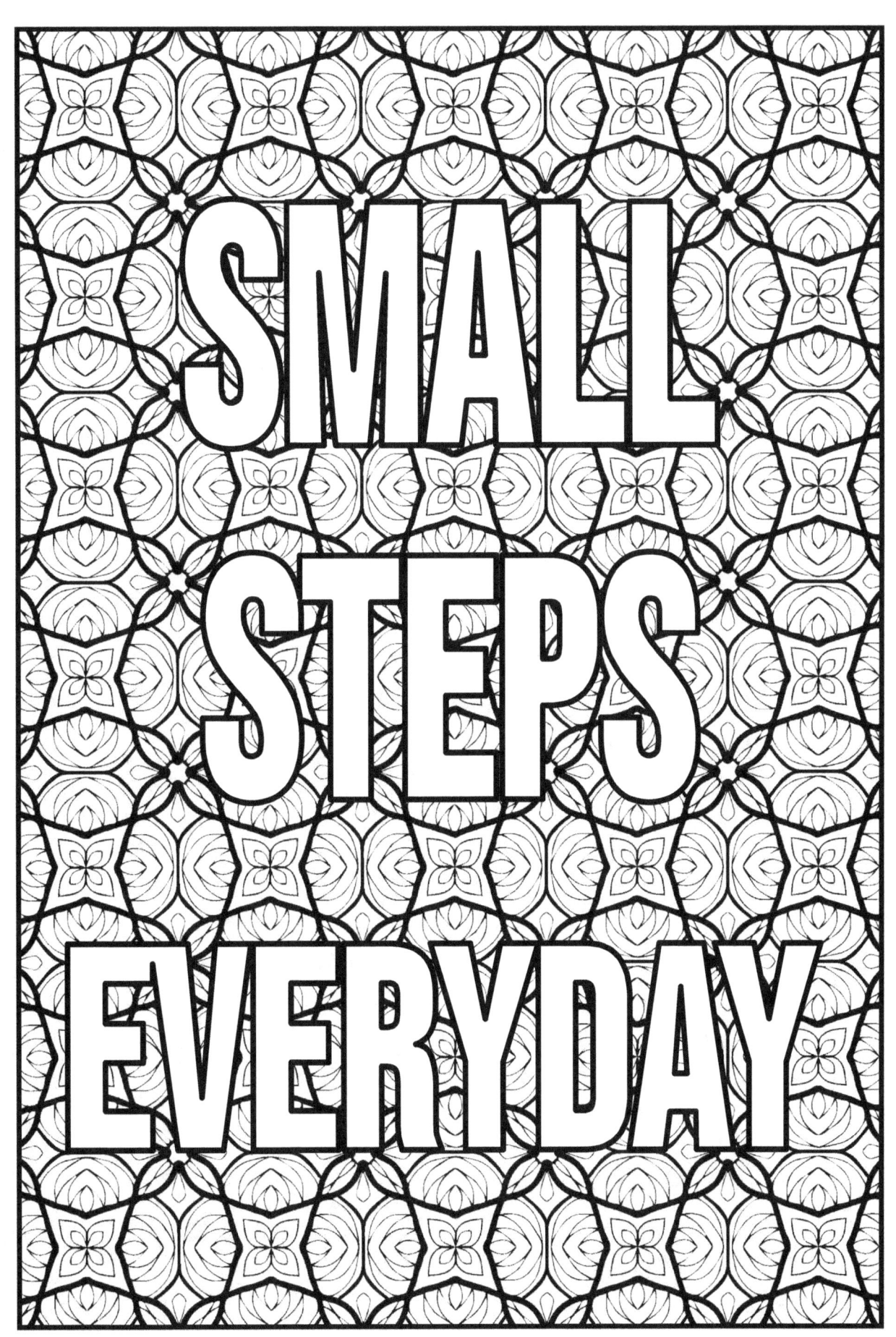

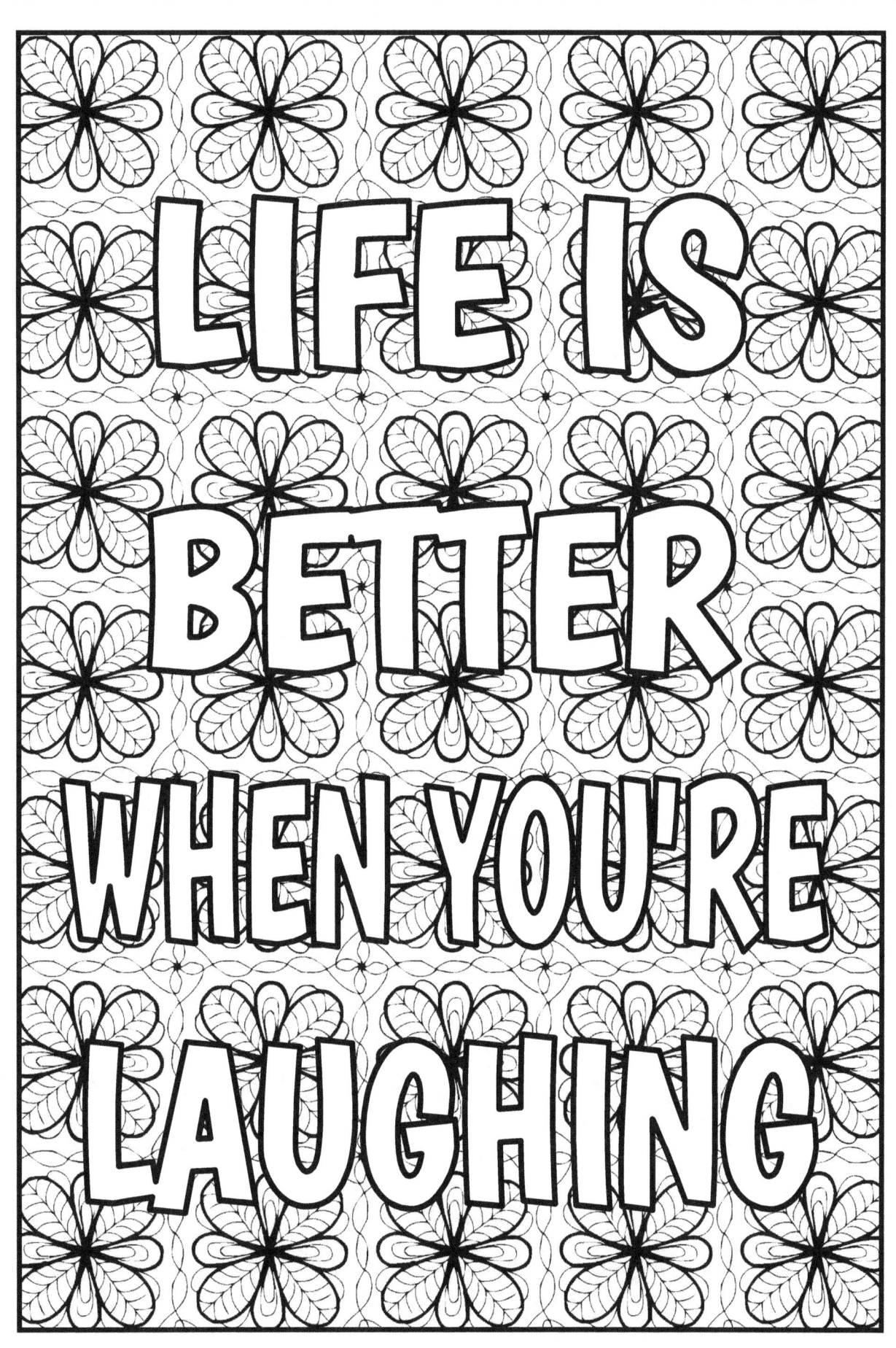

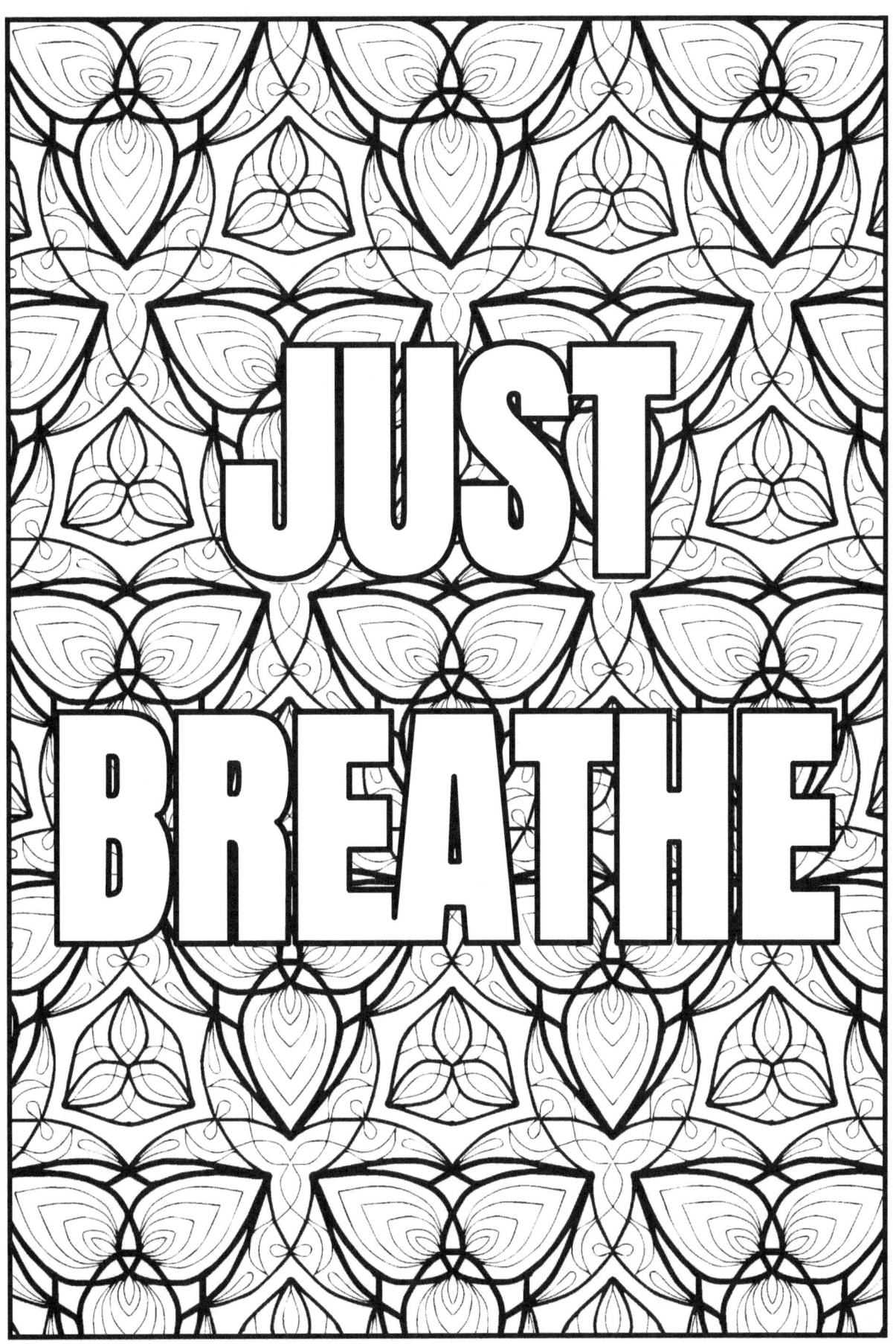

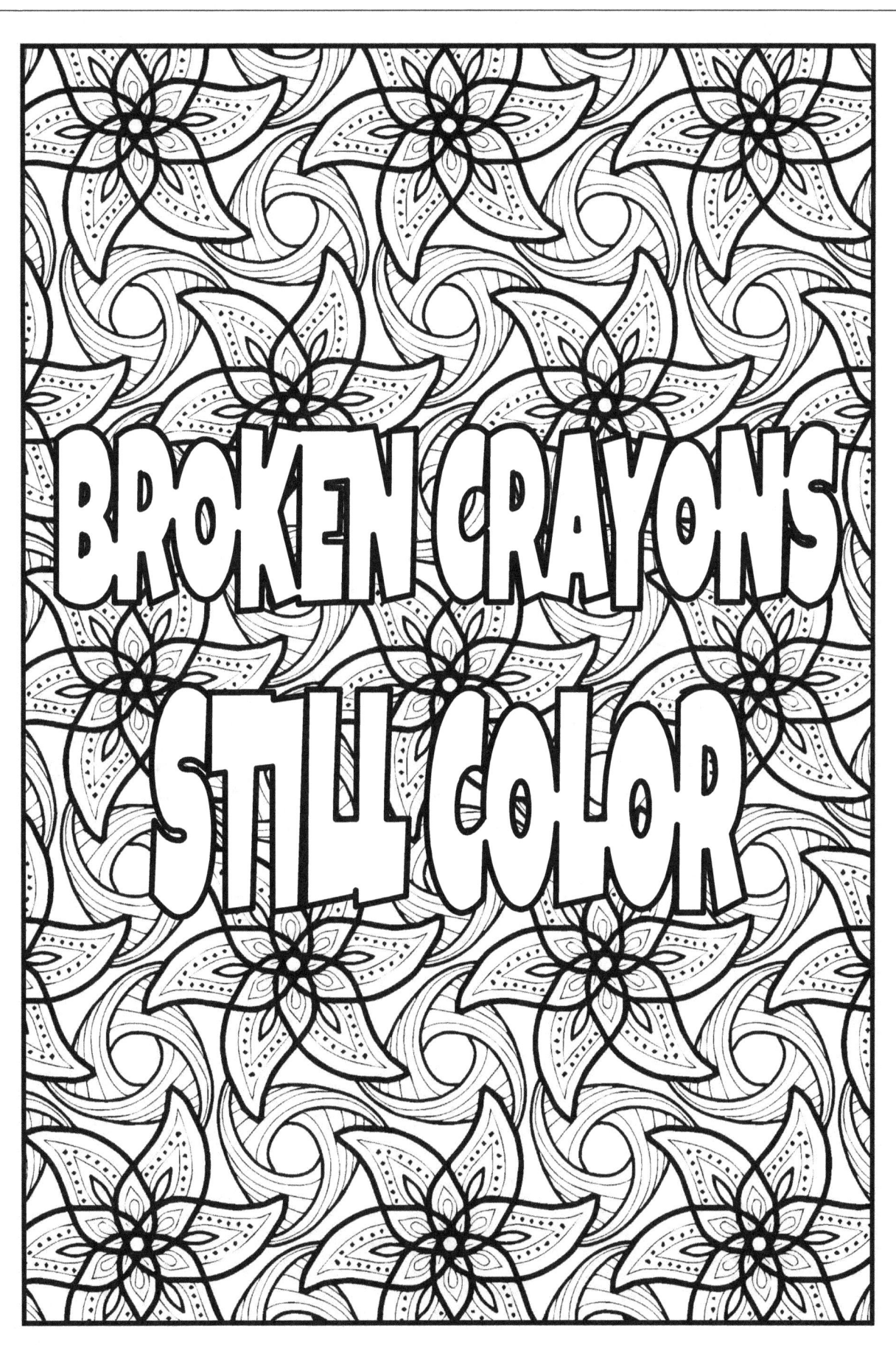

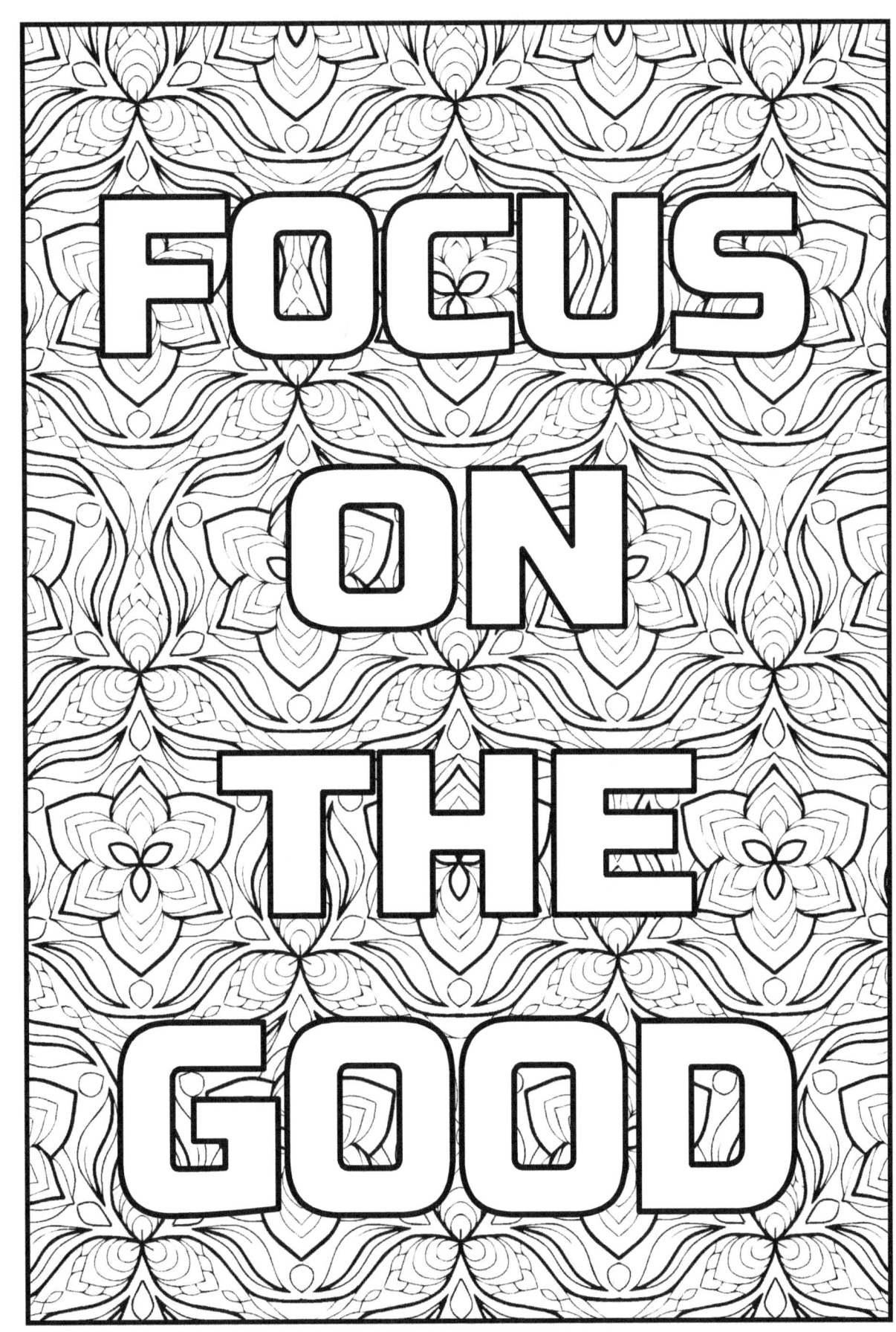

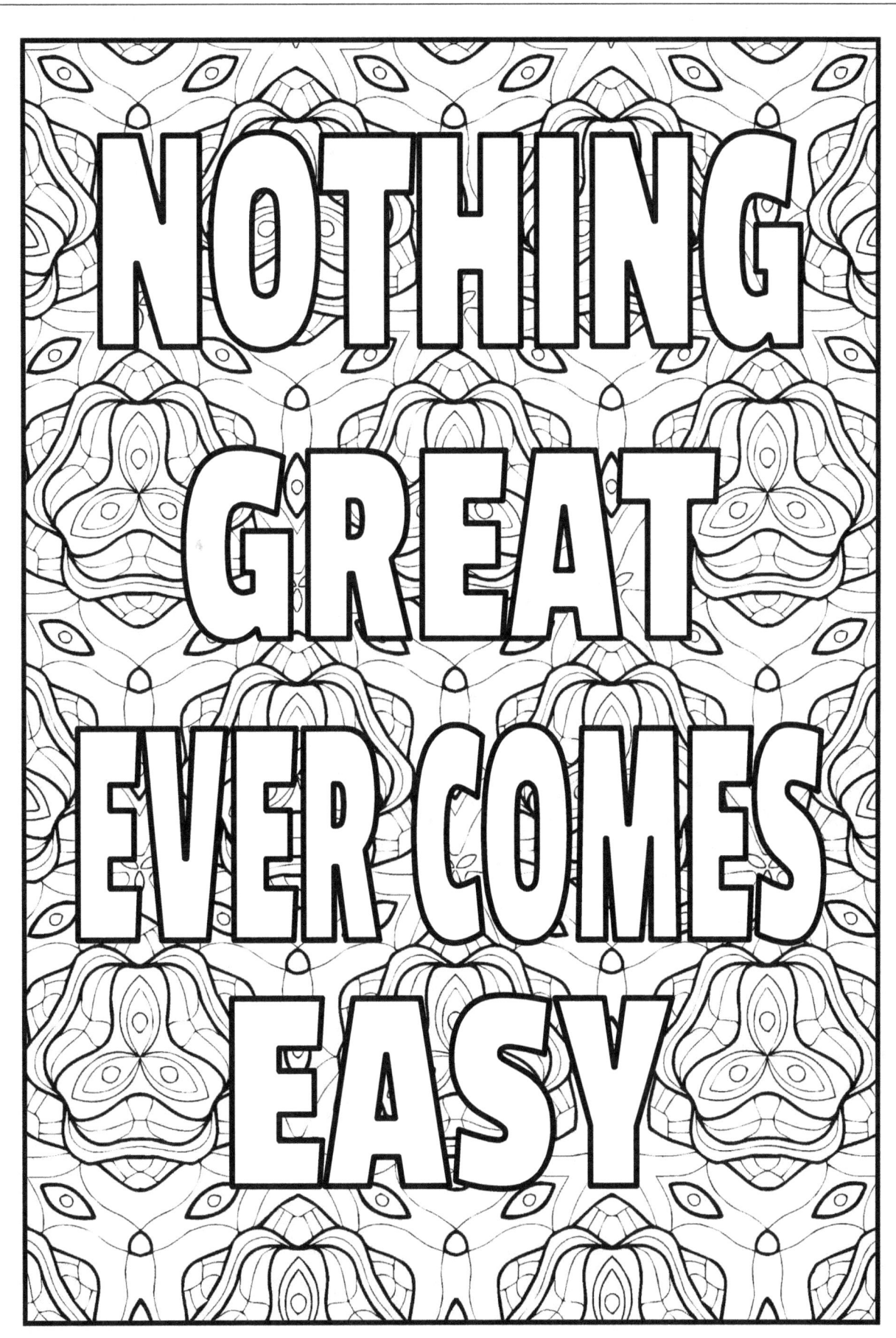

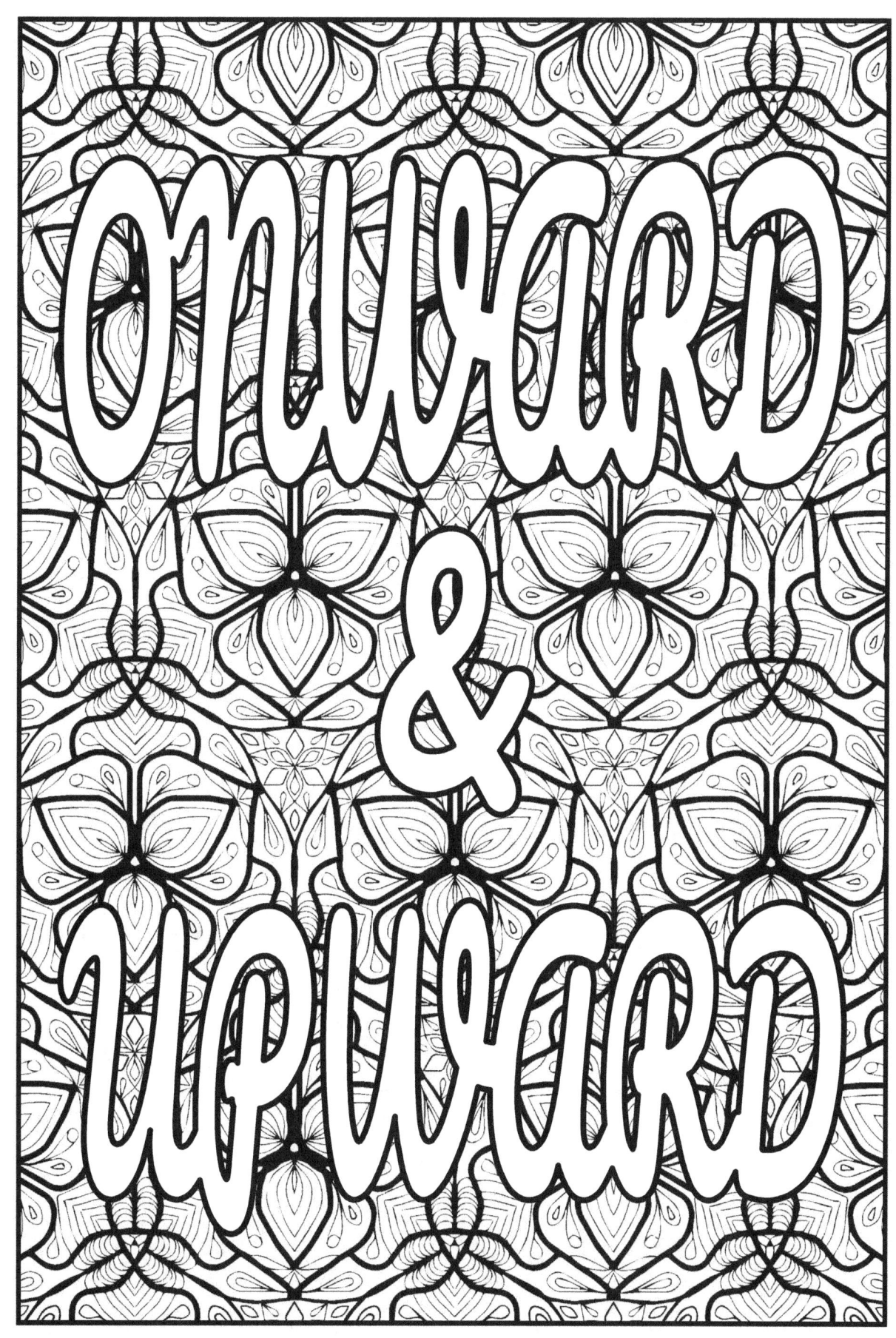

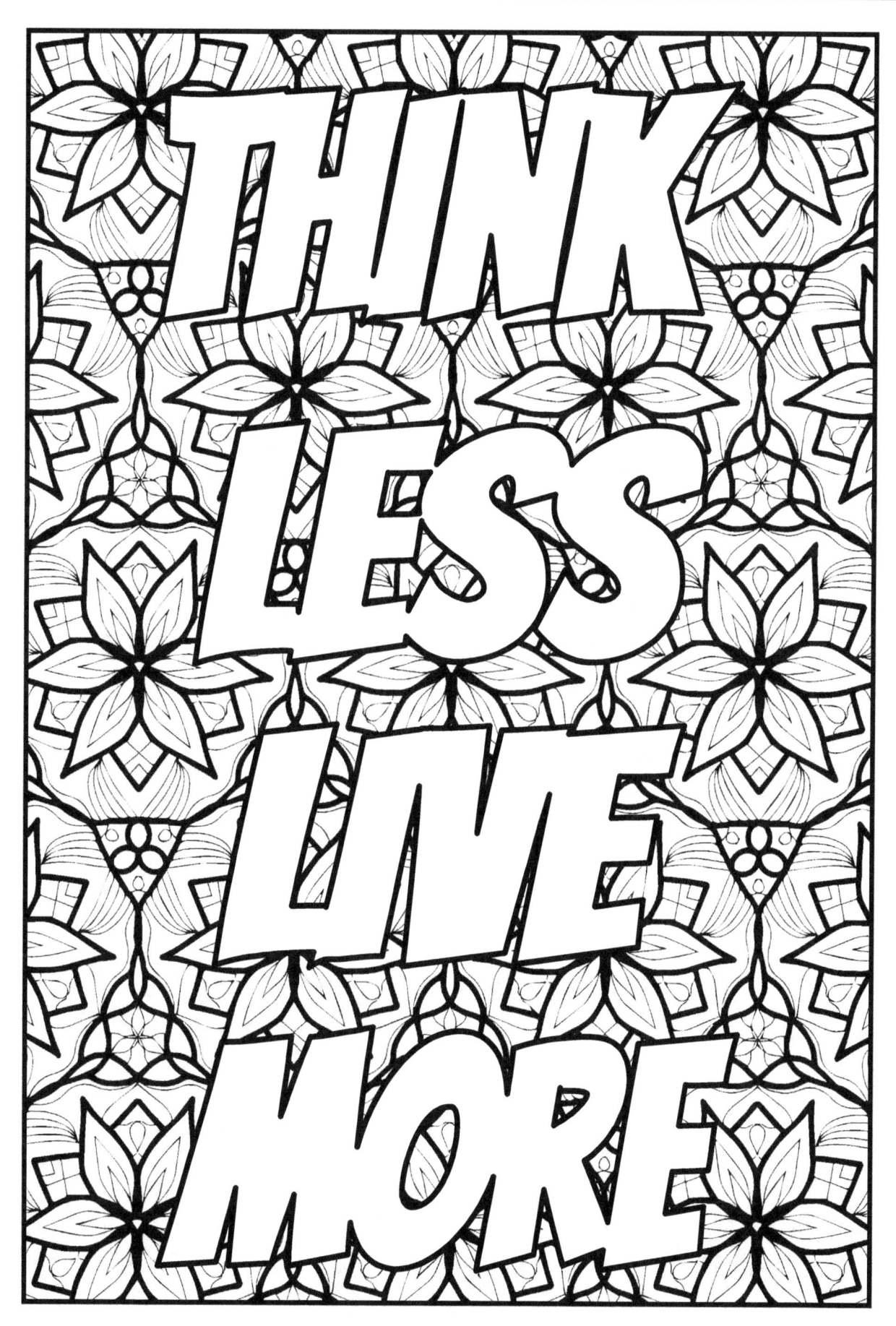

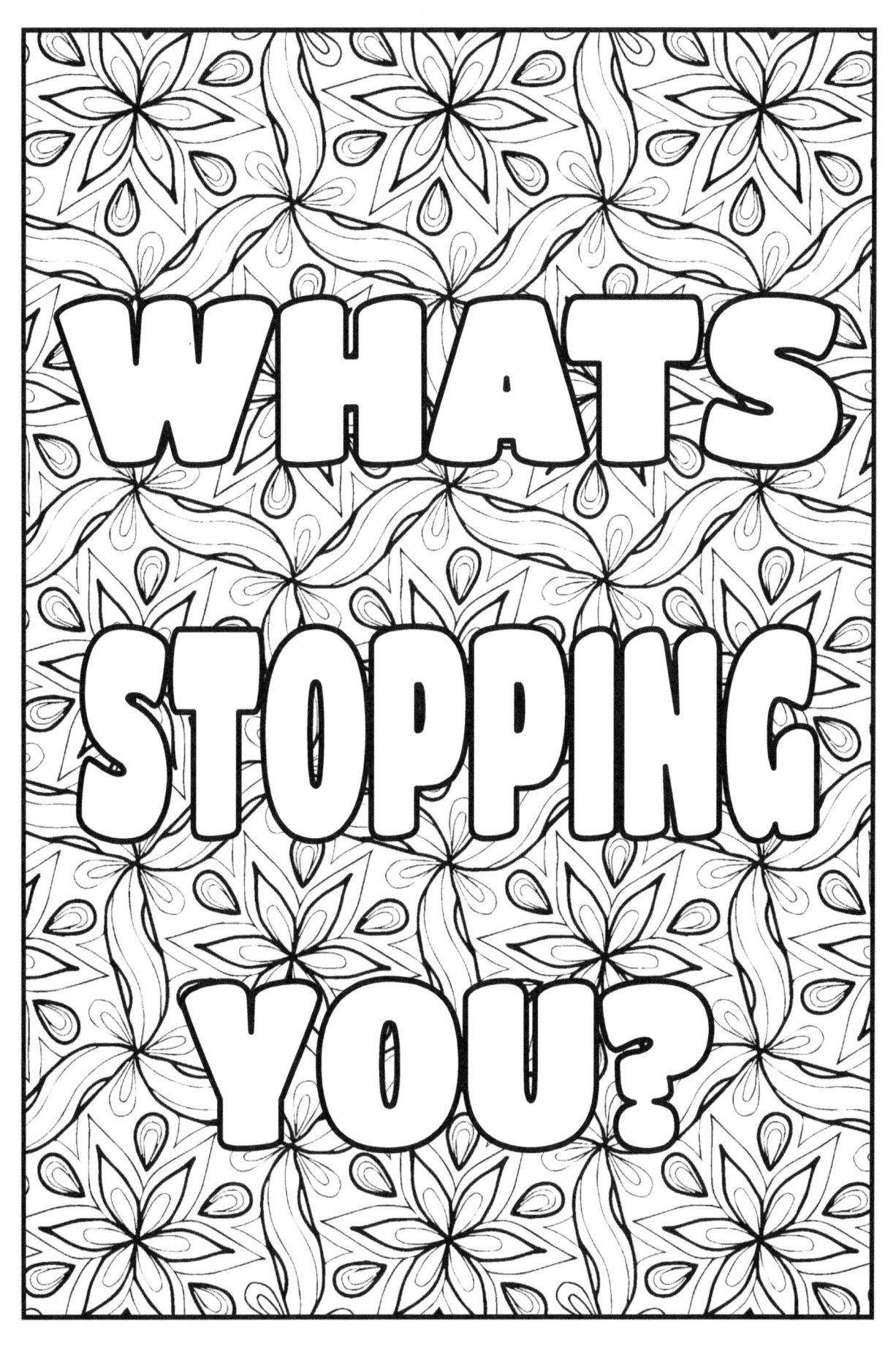

www.ingramcontent.com/pod-product-compliance
Lightning Source LLC
Chambersburg PA
CBHW060435220526
45465CB00008B/3146